experiment
CENTRAL

E l –L volume 2

derstanding scientific principles through projects

John T. Tanacredi & John Loret, General Editors

AN IMPRINT OF THE GALE GROUP

DETROIT · NEW YORK · SAN FRANCISCO
LONDON · BOSTON · WOODBRIDGE, CT

experiment
CENTRAL Understanding Scientific Principles Through Projects

Researched, developed, and illustrated by **Book Builders Incorporated**

John T. Tanacredi, *General Editor*
John Loret, *General Editor*

U•X•L Staff

Allison McNeill, *U•X•L Senior Editor*
Elizabeth Shaw, *U•X•L Associate Editor*
Carol DeKane Nagel, *U•X•L Managing Editor*
Thomas L. Romig, *U•X•L Publisher*
Meggin Condino, *Senior Analyst, New Product Development*

Shalice Shah-Caldwell, *Permissions Associate (Pictures)*

Rita Wimberley, *Senior Buyer*
Evi Seoud, *Assistant Production Manager*
Dorothy Maki, *Manufacturing Manager*
Mary Beth Trimper, *Production Director*

Eric Johnson, Tracey Rowens, *Senior Art Directors*

Pamela A. Reed, *Imaging Coordinator*
Christine O'Bryan, *Graphic Specialist*
Randy Basset, *Image Database Supervisor*
Barbara Yarrow, *Graphic Services Manager*

Linda Mahoney, LM Design, *Typesetting*

Library of Congress Cataloging-in-Publication Data.

Loret, John.
  Experiment central: understanding scientific principles through projects / John Loret,
  John T. Tanacredi.
      p. cm.
  Includes bibliographical references and index.
  Contents: v. 1. A-Ec — v. 2. El-L — v. 3. M-Sc — v. 4. So-Z
  Summary: Demonstrates scientific concepts by means of experiments, including
  step-by-step instructions, lists of materials, troubleshooter's guide, and interpretation and
  explanation of results.
  ISBN 0-7876-2892-1 (set). — ISBN 0-7876-2893-X (v. 1) — ISBN 0-7876-2894-8 (v.2)
  — ISBN 0-7876-2895-6 (v.3) — ISBN 0-7876-2896-4 (v. 4)
  1. Science-Experiments-Juvenile literature. [1. Science-Experiments. 2.
  Experiments.] I. Tanacredi, John T. II. Title.
Q164 .L57 2000
507'.8-dc21   99-054142

contents

Volume 2: El-L

contents

Volume 3: M-Sc

experiment
CENTRAL

Volume 4: So-Z

reader's guide

Experiment Central: Understanding Scientific Principles Through Projects provides in one resource a wide variety of experiments covering nine key science curriculum fields—Astronomy, Biology, Botany, Chemistry, Ecology, Geology, Meteorology, Physics, and Scientific Method—spanning the earth sciences, life sciences, and physical sciences.

One hundred experiments and projects for students are presented in 50 subject-specific chapters. Chapters, each devoted to a scientific concept, include: Acid Rain, Biomes, Chemical Energy, Flight, Greenhouse Effect, Optics, Solar Energy, Stars, Volcanoes, and Weather. Two experiments or projects are provided in each chapter.

Entry format

Chapters are arranged alphabetically by scientific concept and are presented in a standard, easy-to-follow format. All chapters open with an explanatory overview section designed to introduce students to the scientific concept and provide the background behind a concept's discovery or important figures who helped advance the study of the field.

Each experiment is divided into eight standard sections designed to help students follow the experimental process clearly from beginning to end. Sections are:

- Purpose/Hypothesis
- Level of Difficulty
- Materials Needed
- Approximate Budget
- Timetable
- Step-by-Step Instructions
- Summary of Results
- Change the Variables

Each chapter also includes a "Design Your Own Experiment" section that allows students to apply what they have learned about a particular concept and create their own experiments. This section is divided into:

- How to Select a Topic Relating to this Concept
- Steps in the Scientific Method
- Recording Data and Summarizing the Results
- Related Projects

Concluding all chapters is a "For More Information" section that provides students with a list of books with further information about that particular topic.

Special Features

- A "Words to Know" section runs in the margin of each chapter providing definitions of terms used in that chapter. Terms in this list are bolded in the text upon first usage. A cumulative glossary collected from all "Words to Know" sections in the 50 chapters is included in the beginning of each volume.

- **Experiments by Scientific Field** index categorizes all 100 experiments by scientific curriculum area.

- **Parent's and Teacher's Guide** recommends that a responsible adult always oversee a student's experiment and provides several safety guidelines for all students to follow.

- Standard sidebar boxes accompany experiments and projects:

"**What Are the Variables?**" explains the factors that may have an impact on the outcome of a particular experiment.

"**How to Experiment Safely**" clearly explains any risks involved with the experiment and how to avoid them. While all experiments have been constructed with safety in mind, it is always recommended to proceed with caution and work under adult supervision while performing any experiment (please refer to Parent's and Teacher's Guide on page xvii).

"**Troubleshooter's Guide**" presents problems that a student might encounter with an experiment, possible causes of the problem, and ways to remedy the problem.

- **Budget Index** categorizes experiments by approximate cost. Budgets may vary depending on what materials are readily available in the average household.

- **Level of Difficulty Index** lists experiments according to "Easy," "Moderate," "Difficult," or combination thereof. Level of difficulty is determined by such factors as the time necessary to complete the experiment, level of adult supervision recommended, and skill level of the average student. Level of difficulty will vary depending on the student. A teacher or parent should always be consulted before any experiment is attempted.

- **Timetable Index** categorizes each experiment by the time needed to complete it, including set-up and follow-through time. Times given are approximate.

- **General Subject Index** provides access to all major terms, people, places, and topics covered in *Experiment Central.*

- Approximately **150 photographs** enhance the text.

- Approximately **300 drawings** illustrate specific steps in the experiments, helping students follow the experimental procedure.

Acknowledgments

Credit is due to the general editors of *Experiment Central* who lent their time and expertise to the project, and oversaw compilation of the volumes and their contents:

John T. Tanacredi, Ph.D.
Adjunct Full Professor of Ecology
Department of Civil and Environmental Engineering,
Polytechnic University
Adjunct Full Professor of Environmental Sciences,
Nassau Community College, State University of New York
President, The Science Museum of Long Island

John Loret, Ph.D., D.Sc.
Professor Emeritus and Former Director of Environmental
Studies of Queens College, City University of New York
Director, The Science Museum of Long Island

A note of appreciation is extended to the *Experiment Central* advisors, who provided their input when this work was in its formative stages:

reader's guide

Linda Barr
  Editor and Writer for Book Builders Incorporated

Teresa F. Bettac
  Middle School Advanced Science Teacher
  Delaware, Ohio

Linda Leuzzi
  Writer, Trustee of The Science Museum of Long Island

David J. Miller
  Director of Education
  The Science Museum of Long Island

Gracious thanks are also extended to science copyeditor Chris Cavette for his invaluable comments, expertise, and dedication to the project.

Comments and Suggestions

We welcome your comments on *Experiment Central.* Please write: Editors, *Experiment Central,* U•X•L, 27500 Drake Rd., Farmington Hills, Michigan, 48331–3535; call toll free: 1–800–877–4253; fax: 248–414–5043; or send e-mail via http://www.galegroup.com.

parent's and teacher's guide

The experiments and projects in *Experiment Central* have been carefully constructed with issues of safety in mind, but your guidance and supervision are still required. Following the safety guidelines that accompany each experiment and project (found in the "How to Experiment Safely" sidebar box), as well as putting to work the safe practices listed below, will help your child or student avoid accidents. Oversee your child or student during experiments, and make sure he or she follows these safety guidelines:

- Always wear safety goggles if there is any possibility of sharp objects, small particles, splashes of liquid, or gas fumes getting in someone's eyes.

- Always wear protective gloves when handling materials that could irritate the skin.

- Never leave an open flame, such as a lit candle, unattended. Never wear loose clothing around an open flame.

- Follow instructions carefully when using electrical equipment, including batteries, to avoid getting shocked.

- Be cautious when handling sharp objects or glass equipment that might break. Point scissors away from you and use them carefully.

- Always ask for help in cleaning up spills, broken glass, or other hazardous materials.

- Always use protective gloves when handling hot objects. Set them down only on a protected surface that will not be damaged by heat.

- Always wash your hands thoroughly after handling material that might contain harmful microorganisms, such as soil and pond water.

- Do not substitute materials in an experiment without asking a knowledgeable adult about possible reactions.

- Do not use or mix unidentified liquids or powders. The result might be an explosion or poisonous fumes.

- Never taste or eat any substances being used in an experiment.

- Always wear old clothing or a protective apron to avoid staining your clothes.

experiments by scientific field

Chapter name in
brackets, followed
by experiment name;
bold type indicates
volume number, followed
by page number.

Botany

Chemistry

Ecology

experiment
CENTRAL

Geology

Meteorology

Physics

All Subjects

experiments by scientific field

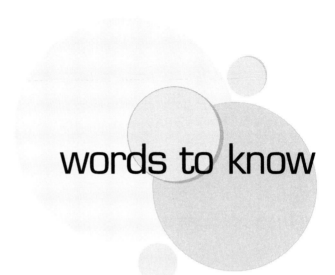

words to know

A

Abscission: The point at which a leaf meets a twig.

Acceleration: The rate at which the velocity and/or direction of an object is changing with the respect to time.

Acid: Substance that when dissolved in water is capable of reacting with a base to form salts and release hydrogen ions.

Acid rain: A form of precipitation that is significantly more acidic than neutral water, often produced as the result of industrial processes.

Acoustics: The science concerned with the production, properties, and propagation of sound waves.

Active solar energy system: A solar energy system that uses pumps or fans to circulate heat captured from the Sun.

Adhesion: Attraction between two different substances.

Aeration: Shaking a liquid to allow trapped gases to escape and to add oxygen.

Aerobic: Requiring oxygen.

Aerodynamics: The study of the motion of gases (particularly air) and the motion and control of objects in the air.

Alga/Algae: Single-celled or multicellular plants or plantlike organisms that contain chlorophyll, thus making their own food by photosynthesis. Algae grow mainly in water.

Alignment: Adjustment to a certain direction or orientation.

Alkaline: Having a pH of more than 7.

Alloy: A mixture of two or more metals with properties different from those metals of which it is made.

Amine: An organic compound derived from ammonia.

Amphibians: Animals that live on land and breathe air but return to the water to reproduce.

Amplitude: The maximum displacement (difference between an original position and a later position) of the material that is vibrating. Amplitude can be thought of visually as the highest and lowest points of a wave.

Anaerobic: Functioning without oxygen.

Anemometer: A device that measures wind speed.

Animalcules: Life forms that Anton van Leeuwenhoek named when he first saw them under his microscope; they later became known as protozoa and bacteria.

Anthocyanin: Red pigment found in leaves, petals, stems, and other parts of a plant.

Antibody: A protein produced by certain cells of the body as an immune (disease-fighting) response to a specific foreign antigen.

Aquifer: Underground layer of sand, gravel, or spongy rock that collects water.

Arch: A curved structure spanning an opening that supports a wall or other weight above the opening.

Artesian well: A well in which water is under pressure.

Asexual reproduction: Any reproductive process that does not involve the union of two individuals in the exchange of genetic material.

Astronomers: Scientists who study the positions, motions, and composition of stars and other objects in the sky.

Astronomy: The study of the physical properties of objects and matter outside Earth's atmosphere.

Atmosphere: Layers of air that surround Earth.

experiment
CENTRAL

Atmospheric pressure: The pressure exerted by the atmosphere at Earth's surface due to the weight of the air.

Atom: The smallest unit of an element, made up of protons and neutrons in a central nucleus surrounded by moving electrons.

Autotroph: An organism that can build all the food and produce all the energy it needs with its own resources.

Auxins: A group of plant hormones responsible for patterns of plant growth.

B

Bacteria: Single-celled microorganisms that live in soil, water, plants, and animals that play a key role in the decaying of organic matter and the cycling of nutrients. Some are agents of disease.

Bacteriology: The scientific study of bacteria, their characteristics, and their activities as related to medicine, industry, and agriculture.

Base: Substance that when dissolved in water is capable of reacting with an acid to form salts and release hydrogen ions; has a pH of more than 7.

Beriberi: A disease caused by a deficiency of thiamine and characterized by nerve and gastrointestinal disorders.

Biochemical oxygen demand (BOD$_5$): The amount of oxygen that microorganisms use over a five-day period in 68° Fahrenheit (20° Celsius) water to decay organic matter.

Biological variables: Living factors such as bacteria, fungi, and animals that can affect the processes that occur in nature and in an experiment.

Biomes: Large geographical areas with specific climates and soils, as well as distinct plant and animal communities that are interdependent.

Bond: The force that holds two atoms together.

Botany: The branch of biology involving the study of plant life.

Braided rivers: Wide, shallow rivers with pebbly islands in the middle.

Buoyancy: The tendency of a fluid to exert a lifting effect on a body immersed in it.

By-products: Something produced in the making of something else.

c

Calibration: Standardizing or adjusting a measuring instrument so its measurements are correct.

Capillary action: The tendency of water to rise through a narrow tube by the force of adhesion between the water and the walls of the tube.

Carbohydrate: A compound consisting of carbon, hydrogen, and oxygen found in plants and used as a food by humans and other animals.

Carnivore: Meat-eating organism.

Carotene: Yellowish-orange pigment present in most leaves.

Catalyst: A compound that speeds up the rate of a chemical reaction without undergoing any change in its own composition.

Celestial: Describing planets or other objects in space.

Cell: The basic unit of a living organism; cells are structured to perform highly specialized functions.

Cell membrane: The thin layer of tissue that surrounds a cell.

Cell theory: The idea that all living things have one or more similar cells that carry out the same functions for the living process.

Centrifuge: A device that rapidly spins a solution so that the heavier components will separate from the lighter ones.

Centripetal force: Rotating force that moves towards the center or axis.

Channel: A shallow trench carved into the ground by the pressure and movement of a river.

Chemical energy: Energy stored in chemical bonds.

Chemical property: A characteristic of a substance that allows it to undergo a chemical change. Chemical properties include flammability and sensitivity to light.

Chemical reaction: Any chemical change in which at least one new substance is formed.

Chlorophyll: A green pigment found in plants that absorbs sunlight, providing the energy used in photosynthesis, or the conversion of carbon dioxide and water to complex carbohydrates.

Chloroplasts: Small structures in plant cells that contain chlorophyll and in which the process of photosynthesis takes place.

Chromatography: A method for separating mixtures into their component parts (into their "ingredients," or into what makes them up).

Circuit: The complete path of an electric current including the source of electric energy.

Cleavage: The tendency of a mineral to split along certain planes.

Climate: The average weather that a region experiences over a long period.

Coagulation: The clumping together of particles in a liquid.

Cohesion: Attraction between like substances.

Colloid: A mixture containing particles suspended in, but not dissolved in, a dispersing medium.

Colony: A mass of microorganisms that have been bred in a medium.

Combustion: Any chemical reaction in which heat, and usually light, is produced. It is commonly the burning of organic substances during which oxygen from the air is used to form carbon dioxide and water vapor.

Complete metamorphosis: Metamorphosis in which a larva becomes a pupa before changing into an adult form.

Composting: The process in which organic compounds break down and become dark, fertile soil called humus.

Concave: Hollowed or rounded upward, like the inside of a bowl; arched.

Concentration: The amount of a substance present in a given volume, such as the number of molecules in a liter.

Condense/condensation: The process by which a gas changes into a liquid.

Conduction: The flow of heat through a solid.

Confined aquifer: An aquifer with a layer of impermeable rock above it; the water is held under pressure.

Coniferous: Refers to trees, such as pines and firs, that bear cones and have needle-like leaves that are not shed all at once.

Constellations: Eighty-eight patterns of stars in the night sky.

Continental drift: The theory that continents move apart slowly at a predictable rate.

Control experiment: A set-up that is identical to the experiment but is not affected by the variable that will be changed during the experiment.

Convection: The circulatory motion that occurs in a gas or liquid at a nonuniform temperature; the variation of the motion is caused by the substance's density and the action of gravity.

Convection current: Circular movement of a fluid in response to alternating heating and cooling.

Convex: Curved or rounded like the outside of a ball.

Corona: The outermost atmospheric layer of the Sun.

Corrosion: An oxidation-reduction reaction in which a metal is oxidized (reacted with oxygen) and oxygen is reduced, usually in the presence of moisture.

Cotyledon: Seed leaves, which contain stored food for the embryo.

Crust: The hard, outer shell of Earth that floats upon the softer, denser mantle.

Cultures: Microorganisms growing in prepared nutrients.

Cyanobacteria: Oxygen-producing, aquatic bacteria capable of manufacturing its own food; resembles algae.

Cycle: Occurrence of events that take place the same time every year; a single complete vibration.

Cytology: The branch of biology concerned with the study of cells.

Cytoplasm: The semifluid substance inside a cell that surrounds the nucleus and the other membrane-enclosed organelles.

D

Decanting: The process of separating a suspension by waiting for its heavier components to settle out and then pouring off the lighter ones.

Decibel (dB): A unit of measurement for sound.

Deciduous: Plants that lose their leaves at some season of the year, and then grow them back at another season.

Decomposition: The breakdown of complex molecules—molecules of which dead organisms are composed—into simple nutrients that can be reutilized by living organisms.

Decomposition reaction: A chemical reaction in which one substance is broken down into two or more substances.

Denaturization: Altering of an enzyme so it no longer works.

Density: The mass of a substance compared to its volume.

Density ball: A ball with the fixed standard of 1.0 g/l, which is the exact density of pure water.

Dependent variable: The variable in a function whose value depends on the value of another variable in the function.

Deposition: Dropping of sediments that occurs when a river loses its energy of motion.

Desert: A biome with a hot-to-cool climate and dry weather.

Desertification: Transformation of arid or semiarid productive land into desert.

Dewpoint: The point at which water vapor begins to condense.

Dicot: Plants with a pair of embryonic seeds that appear at germination.

Diffraction: The bending of light or another form of electromagnetic radiation as it passes through a tiny hole or around a sharp edge.

Diffraction grating: A device consisting of a surface into which are etched very fine, closely spaced grooves that cause different wavelengths of light to reflect or refract (bend) by different amounts.

Diffusion: Random movement of molecules that leads to a net movement of molecules from a region of high concentration to a region of low concentration.

Disinfection: Using chemicals to kill harmful organisms.

Dissolved oxygen (DO): Oxygen molecules that have dissolved in water.

Distillation: The process of separating liquids from solids or from other liquids with different boiling points by a method of evaporation and condensation, so that each component in a mixture can be collected separately in its pure form.

DNA: Abbreviation for deoxyribonucleic acid. Large, complex molecules found in nuclei of cells that carry genetic information for an organism's development.

Domain: Small regions in an iron object that possess their own magnetic charges.

Dormancy: A state of inactivity in an organism.

Dormant: Describing an inactive organism.

Drought: A prolonged period of dry weather that damages crops or prevents their growth.

Dry cell: An electrolytic cell or battery using a non-liquid electrolyte.

Dynamic equilibrium: A situation in which substances are moving into and out of cell walls at an equal rate.

E

Earthquake: An unpredictable event in which masses of rock shift below Earth's surface, releasing enormous amounts of energy and sending out shock waves that sometimes cause the ground to shake dramatically.

Eclipse: A phenomenon in which the light from a celestial body is temporarily cut off by the presence of another body.

Ecologists: Scientists who study the interrelationship of organisms and their environments.

Ecosystem: An ecological community, including plants, animals and microorganisms considered together with their environment.

Electric charge repulsion: Repulsion of particles caused by a layer of negative ions surrounding each particle. The repulsion prevents coagulation and promotes the even dispersion of such particles through a mixture.

Electrical energy: The motion of electrons within any object that conducts electricity.

experiment
CENTRAL

Electricity: A form of energy caused by the presence of electrical charges in matter.

Electrode: A material that will conduct an electrical current, usually a metal; used to carry electrons into or out of an electrochemical cell.

Electrolyte: Any substance that, when dissolved in water, conducts an electric current.

Electromagnetic spectrum: The complete array of electromagnetic radiation, including radio waves (at the longest-wavelength end), microwaves, infrared radiation, visible light, ultraviolet radiation, X rays, and gamma rays (at the shortest-wavelength end).

Electromagnetic waves: Radiation that has properties of both an electric and a magnetic wave and that travels through a vacuum at the speed of light.

Electromagnetism: A form of magnetic energy produced by the flow of an electric current through a metal core. Also, the study of electric and magnetic fields and their interaction with charges and currents.

Electron: A subatomic particle with a mass of about one atomic mass unit and a single electrical charge that orbits the nucleus of an atom.

Electroscope: A device that determines whether an object is electrically charged.

Elevation: Height above sea level.

Elliptical: An orbital path that is egg-shaped or resembles an elongated circle.

Embryo: The seed of a plant, which through germination can develop into a new plant; also, the earliest stage of animal development.

Embryonic: The earliest stages of development.

Endothermic reaction: A chemical reaction that absorbs energy, such as photosynthesis, the production of food by plant cells.

Energy: The ability to cause an action or for work to be done. Also, power that can be used to perform work, such as solar energy.

Environmental variables: Nonliving factors such as air temperature, water, pollution, and pH that can affect processes that occur in nature and in an experiment.

Enzymes: Any of numerous complex proteins produced by living cells that act as catalysts, speeding up the rate of chemical reactions in living organisms.

Enzymology: The science of studying enzymes.

Ephemerals: Plants that lie dormant in dry soil for years until major rainstorms occur.

Epicenter: The location where the seismic waves of an earthquake first appear on the surface, usually almost directly above the focus.

Equilibrium: A process in which the rates at which various changes take place balance each other, resulting in no overall change.

Erosion: The process by which topsoil is carried away by water, wind, or ice.

Eutrophic zone: The upper part of the ocean where sunlight penetrates, supporting plant life such as phytoplankton.

Eutrophication: Natural process by which a lake or other body of water becomes enriched in dissolved nutrients, spurring aquatic plant growth.

Evaporate/evaporation: The process by which liquid changes into a gas; also, the escape of water vapor into the air, yielding only the solute.

Exothermic reaction: A chemical reaction that releases energy, such as the burning of fuel.

Experiment: A controlled observation.

F

Fat: A type of lipid, or chemical compound used as a source of energy, to provide insulation, and to protect organs in an animal's body.

Fault: A crack running through rock that is the result of tectonic forces.

Fault blocks: Pieces of rock from Earth's crust that overlap and cause earthquakes when they press together and snap from pressure.

Filtration: The use of a screen or filter to separate larger particles from smaller ones that can slip through the filter's openings.

experiment
CENTRAL

Fluorescence: Luminescence (glowing) that stops within 10 nanoseconds after an energy source has been removed.

Focal length: The distance of a focus from the surface of a lens or concave mirror.

Focal point: The point at which rays of light converge (come together) or from which they diverge (move apart).

Food web: An interconnected set of all the food chains in the same ecosystem.

Force: A physical interaction (pushing or pulling) tending to change the state of motion (velocity) of an object.

Fossil fuel: A fuel such as coal, oil, or natural gas that is formed over millions of years from the remains of plants and animals.

Fracture: A mineral's tendency to break into curved, rough, or jagged surfaces.

Frequency: The rate at which vibrations take place (number of times per second the motion is repeated), given in cycles per second or in hertz (Hz). Also, the number of waves that pass a given point in a given period of time.

Front: The front edges of moving masses of air.

Fungus: Kingdom of various single-celled or multicellular organisms, including mushrooms, molds, yeasts, and mildews, that do not contain chlorophyll. (Plural is fungi.)

Fusion: Combining of nuclei of two or more lighter elements into one nucleus of a heavier element; the process stars use to produce energy to support themselves against their own gravity.

G

Galaxy: A large collection of stars and clusters of stars containing anywhere from a few million to a few trillion stars.

Gene: A segment of a DNA (deoxyribonucleic acid) molecule contained in the nucleus of a cell that acts as a kind of code for the production of some specific protein. Genes carry instructions for the formation, functioning, and transmission of specific traits from one generation to another.

Genetic material: Material that transfers characteristics from a parent to its offspring.

Geology: The study of the origin, history, and structure of Earth.

Geotropism: The tendency of roots to bend toward Earth.

Germ theory of disease: The belief that disease is caused by germs.

Germination: The beginning of growth of a seed.

Gibbous moon: A phase of the Moon when more than half of its surface is lighted.

Glacier: A large mass of ice formed from snow that has packed together and which moves slowly down a slope under its own weight.

Global warming: Warming of Earth's atmosphere that results from an increase in the concentration of gases that store heat such as carbon dioxide.

Glucose: Also known as blood sugar; a simple sugar broken down in cells to produce energy.

Golgi body: Organelle that sorts, modifies, and packages molecules.

Gravity: Force of attraction between objects, the strength of which depends on the mass of each object and the distance between them.

Greenhouse effect: The warming of Earth's atmosphere due to water vapor, carbon dioxide, and other gases in the atmosphere that trap heat radiated from Earth's surface.

Greenhouse gases: Gases that absorb infrared radiation and warm air before it escapes into space.

Groundwater: Water that soaks into the ground and is stored in the small spaces between the rocks and soil.

H

Heat: A form of energy produced by the motion of molecules that make up a substance.

Heat energy: The energy produced when two substances that have different temperatures are combined.

Herbivore: Plant-eating organism.

Hertz (Hz): The unit of frequency; a measure of the number of waves that pass a given point per second of time.

Heterotrophs: Organisms that cannot make their own food and that must, therefore, obtain their food from other organisms.

High air pressure: An area where the air molecules are more dense.

Hormone: A chemical produced in living cells that regulates the functions of the organism.

Humidity: The amount of water vapor (moisture) contained in the air.

Humus: Fragrant, spongy, nutrient-rich decayed plant or animal matter.

Hydrologic cycle: Continual movement of water from the atmosphere to Earth's surface through precipitation and back to the atmosphere through evaporation and transpiration.

Hydrologists: Scientists who study water and its cycle.

Hydrology: The study of water and its cycle.

Hydrometer: An instrument that determines the specific gravity of a liquid.

Hydrophilic: A substance that is attracted to and readily mixes with water.

Hydrophobic: A substance that is repelled by and does not mix with water.

Hydrotropism: The tendency of roots to grow toward a water source.

Hypertonic solution: A solution with a higher osmotic pressure (solute concentration) than another solution.

Hypothesis: An idea in the form of a statement that can be tested by observation and/or experiment.

Hypotonic solution: A solution with a lower osmotic pressure (solute concentration) than another solution.

I

Igneous rock: Rock formed from the cooling and hardening of magma.

Immiscible: Incapable of being mixed.

Impermeable: Not allowing substances to pass through.

Impurities: Chemicals or other pollutants in water.

Incomplete metamorphosis: Metamorphosis in which a nymph form gradually becomes an adult through molting.

Independent variable: The variable in a function that determines the final value of the function.

Indicator: Pigments that change color when they come into contact with acidic or basic solutions.

Inertia: The tendency of an object to continue in its state of motion.

Infrared radiation: Electromagnetic radiation of a wavelength shorter than radio waves but longer than visible light that takes the form of heat.

Inner core: Very dense, solid center of Earth.

Inorganic: Not made of or coming from living things.

Insulated wire: Electrical wire coated with a nonconducting material such as plastic.

Insulation/insulator: A material that does not conduct heat or electricity.

Interference fringes: Bands of color that fan around an object.

Ion: An atom or group of atoms that carries an electrical charge—either positive or negative—as a result of losing or gaining one or more electrons.

Ionic conduction: The flow of an electrical current by the movement of charged particles, or ions.

Isobars: Continuous lines on a map that connect areas with the same air pressure.

Isotonic solutions: Two solutions that have the same concentration of solute particles and therefore the same osmotic pressure.

K

Kinetic energy: Energy of an object or system due to its motion.

L

Lactobacilli: A strain of bacteria.

Larva: Immature form (wormlike in insects; fishlike in amphibians) of an organism capable of surviving on its own. A larva does not resemble the parent and must go through metamorphosis, or change, to reach its adult stage.

Lava: Molten rock that occurs at the surface of Earth, usually through volcanic eruptions.

Lens: A piece of transparent material with two curved surfaces that bring together and focus rays of light passing through it.

Lichen: An organism composed of a fungus and a photosynthetic organism in a symbiotic relationship.

Lift: Upper force on the wings of an aircraft created by differences in air pressure on top of and underneath the wings.

Light-year: Distance light travels in one year in the vacuum of space, roughly 5.9 trillion miles (9.5 trillion km).

The Local Group: A cluster of 30 galaxies, including the Milky Way, pulled together gravitationally.

Low air pressure: An area where the air molecules are less dense.

Lunar eclipse: Eclipse that occurs when Earth passes between the Sun and the Moon, casting a shadow on the Moon.

Luster: A glow of reflected light; a sheen.

M

Macroorganisms: Visible organisms that aid in breaking down organic matter.

Magma: Molten rock deep within Earth that consists of liquids, gases, and particles of rocks and crystals. Magma underlies areas of volcanic activity and at Earth's surface is called lava.

Magma chambers: Pools of bubbling liquid rock that are the energy sources causing volcanoes to be active.

Magma surge: A swell or rising wave of magma caused by the movement and friction of tectonic plates; the surge heats and melts rock, adding to the magma and its force.

Magnet: A material that attracts other like material, especially metals.

Magnetic circuit: A series of magnetic domains aligned in the same direction.

Magnetic field: The space around an electric current or a magnet in which a magnetic force can be observed.

Magnetism: A fundamental force of nature caused by the motion of electrons in an atom. Magnetism is manifested by the attraction of certain materials for iron.

Mantle: Thick, dense layer of rock that underlies Earth's crust and overlies the core.

Manure: The waste matter of animals.

Mass: Measure of the total amount of matter in an object. Also, an object's quantity of matter as shown by its gravitational pull on another object.

Matter: Anything that has mass and takes up space.

Meandering river: A lowland river that twists and turns along its route to the sea.

Medium: A material that carries the acoustic vibrations away from the body producing them.

Meniscus: The curved surface of a column of liquid.

Metamorphic rock: Rock formed by transformation of pre-existing rock through changes in temperature and pressure.

Metamorphosis: Transformation of an immature animal into an adult.

Meteorologists: Scientists who study weather and weather forecasting.

Microbiology: Branch of biology dealing with microscopic forms of life.

Microclimate: A local climate.

Microorganisms: Living organisms so small that they can be seen only with the aid of a microscope.

Micropyle: Seed opening that enables water to enter easily.

Milky Way: The galaxy in which our solar system is located.

Mineral: An inorganic substance found in nature with a definite chemical composition and structure. As a nutrient, helps build bones and soft tissues and regulates body functions.

Mixtures: Combinations of two or more substances that are not chemically combined with each other and can exist in any proportion.

Molecule: The smallest particle of a substance that retains all the properties of the substance and is composed of one or more atoms.

Molting: Shedding of the outer layer of an animal, as occurs during growth of insect larvae.

Monocot: Plants with a single embryonic seed at germination.

Moraine: Mass of boulders, stones, and other rock debris carried along and deposited by a glacier.

Multicellular: Living things with many cells joined together.

N

Nanometer: A unit of length; this measurement is equal to one-billionth of a meter.

Nansen bottles: Self-closing containers with thermometers that draw in water at different depths.

Nebula: Bright or dark cloud, often composed of gases and dust, hovering in the space between the stars.

Neutralization: A chemical process in which the mixing of an acidic solution with a basic (alkaline) solution results in a solution that has the properties of neither an acid nor a base.

Neutron: A subatomic particle with a mass of about one atomic mass unit and no electrical charge that is found in the nucleus of an atom.

Niche: The specific role that an organism carries out in its ecosystem.

Nonpoint source: An unidentified source of pollution; may actually be a number of sources.

Nucleus: The central core of an atom, consisting of protons and (usually) neutrons.

Nutrient: A substance needed by an organism in order for it to survive, grow, and develop.

Nutrition: The study of the food nutrients an organism needs in order to maintain well-being.

Nymph: An immature form in the life cycle of insects that go through an incomplete metamorphosis.

o

Oceanography: The study of the chemistry of the oceans, as well as their currents, marine life, and the ocean bed.

Optics: The study of the nature of light and its properties.

Organelles: Membrane-bounded cellular "organs" performing a specific set of functions within a eukaryotic cell.

Organic: Made of or coming from living things.

Osmosis: The movement of fluids and substances dissolved in liquids across a semipermeable membrane from an area of its greater concentration to an area of its lesser concentration until all substances involved reach a balance.

Outer core: A liquid core that surrounds Earth's solid inner core; made mostly of iron.

Oxidation: A chemical reaction in which oxygen reacts with some other substance and in which ions, atoms, or molecules lose electrons.

Oxidation-reduction reaction: A chemical reaction in which one substance loses one or more electrons and the other substance gains one or more electrons.

Oxidation state: The sum of an atom's positive and negative charges.

Oxidizing agent: A chemical substance that gives up oxygen or takes on electrons from another substance.

Ozone layer: The atmospheric layer of approximately 15 to 30 miles (24 to 48 km) above Earth's surface in which the concentration of ozone is significantly higher than in other parts of the atmosphere and that protects the lower atmosphere from harmful solar radiation.

P

Papain: An enzyme obtained from the fruit of the papaya used as a meat tenderizer, as a drug to clean cuts and wounds, and as a digestive aid for stomach disorders.

Passive solar energy system: A solar energy system in which the heat of the Sun is captured, used, and stored by means of the design of a building and the materials from which it is made.

Pasteurization: The process of slow heating that kills bacteria and other microorganisms.

Penicillin: A mold from the fungi group of microorganisms used as an antibiotic.

Pepsin: Digestive enzyme that breaks down protein.

Percolate: To pass through a permeable substance.

Permeable: Having pores that permit a liquid or a gas to pass through.

pH: Abbreviation for potential hydrogen. A measure of the acidity or alkalinity of a solution determined by the concentration of hydrogen ions present in a liter of a given fluid. The pH scale ranges from 0 (greatest concentration of hydrogen ions and therefore most acidic) to 14 (least concentration of hydrogen ions and therefore most alkaline), with 7 representing a neutral solution, such as pure water.

Pharmacology: The science dealing with the properties, reactions, and therapeutic values of drugs.

Phases: Changes in the illuminated Moon surfaces as the Moon revolves around Earth.

Phloem: Plant tissue consisting of elongated cells that transport carbohydrates and other nutrients.

Phosphorescence: Luminescence (glowing) that stops within 10 nanoseconds after an energy source has been removed.

Photoelectric effect: The phenomenon in which light falling upon certain metals stimulates the emission of electrons and changes light into electricity.

Photosynthesis: Chemical process by which plants containing chlorophyll use sunlight to manufacture their own food by converting carbon dioxide and water to carbohydrates, releasing oxygen as a by-product.

Phototropism: The tendency of a plant to grow toward a source of light.

Photovoltaic cells: A device made of silicon that converts sunlight into electricity.

Physical change: A change in which the substance keeps its identity, such as a piece of chalk that has been ground up.

Physical property: A characteristic that you can detect with your senses, such as color and shape.

Phytoplankton: Microscopic aquatic plants that live suspended in the water.

Pigment: A substance that displays a color because of the wavelengths of light that it reflects.

Pitch: A property of a sound, determined by its frequency; the highness or lowness of a sound.

Plates: Large regions of Earth's surface, composed of the crust and uppermost mantle, which move about, forming many of Earth's major geologic surface features.

Pnematocysts: Stinging cells.

Point source: An identified source of pollution.

Pollination: The transfer of pollen from the male reproductive organs to the female reproductive organs of plants.

Pore: An opening or space.

Potential energy: The energy possessed by a body as a result of its position.

Precipitation: Water in its liquid or frozen form when it falls from clouds as rain, snow, sleet, or hail.

Probe: The terminal of a voltmeter, used to connect the voltmeter to a circuit.

Producer: An organism that can manufacture its own food from nonliving materials and an external energy source, usually by photosynthesis.

Product: A compound that is formed as a result of a chemical reaction.

Prominences: Masses of glowing gas, mainly hydrogen, that rise from the Sun's surface like flames.

Propeller: Radiating blades mounted on a quickly rotating shaft that are used to move aircraft forward.

Protein: A complex chemical compound that consists of many amino acids attached to each other that are essential to the structure and functioning of all living cells.

Protists: Members of the kingdom Protista, primarily single-celled organisms that are not plants or animals.

Proton: A subatomic particle with a mass of about one atomic mass unit and a single negative electrical change that is found in the nucleus of an atom.

Protozoan: Single-celled animal-like microscopic organisms that live by taking in food rather than making it by photosynthesis and must live in the presence of water. (Plural is protozoa.)

Pupa: A stage in the metamorphosis of an insect during which its tissues are completely reorganized to take on their adult shape.

R

Radiation: Energy transmitted in the form of electromagnetic waves or subatomic particles.

Radicule: A seed's root system.

Radio wave: Longest form of electromagnetic radiation, measuring up to 6 miles (9.6 km) from peak to peak.

Radiosonde balloons: Instruments for collecting data in the atmosphere and then transmitting that data back to Earth by means of radio waves.

Reactant: A compound present at the beginning of a chemical reaction.

Reaction: Response to an action prompted by a stimulus.

Reduction: A process in which a chemical substance gives off oxygen or takes on electrons.

Reflection: The bouncing of light rays in a regular pattern off the surface of an object.

Refraction: The bending of light rays as they pass at an angle from one transparent or clear medium into a second one of different density.

Rennin: Enzyme used in making cheese.

Resistance: A partial or complete limiting of the flow of electrical current through a material.

Respiration: The physical process that supplies oxygen to living cells and the chemical reactions that take place inside the cells.

Resultant: A force that results from the combined action of two other forces.

Retina: The light-sensitive part of the eyeball that receives images and transmits visual impulses through the optic nerve to the brain.

River: A main course of water into which many other smaller bodies of water flow.

Rock: Naturally occurring solid mixture of minerals.

Runoff: Water in excess of what can be absorbed by the ground.

S

Salinity: The amount of salts dissolved in seawater.

Saturated: Containing the maximum amount of a solute for a given amount of solvent at a certain temperature.

Scientific method: Collecting evidence meticulously and then theorizing from it.

Scribes: Ancient scholars.

Scurvy: A disease caused by a deficiency of vitamin C, which causes a weakening of connective tissue in bone and muscle.

Sediment: Sand, silt, clay, rock, gravel, mud, or other matter that has been transported by flowing water.

Sedimentary rock: Rock formed from the compressed and solidified layers of organic or inorganic matter.

Sedimentation: A process during which gravity pulls particles out of a liquid.

Seismic belt: Boundaries where Earth's plates meet.

Seismic waves: Classified as body waves or surface waves, vibrations in rock and soil that transfer the force of the earthquake from the focus (center) into the surrounding area.

Seismograph: A device that records vibrations of the ground and within Earth.

Seismology: The study and measurement of earthquakes.

Seismometer: A seismograph that measures the movement of the ground.

Semipermeable membrane: A thin barrier between two solutions that permits only certain components of the solutions, usually the solvent, to pass through.

Sexual reproduction: A reproductive process that involves the union of two individuals in the exchange of genetic material.

Silt: Medium-sized soil particles.

Solar collector: A device that absorbs sunlight and collects solar heat.

Solar eclipse: Eclipse that occurs when the Moon passes between Earth and the Sun, casting a shadow on Earth.

Solar energy: Any form of electromagnetic radiation that is emitted by the Sun.

Solute: The substance that is dissolved to make a solution and exists in the least amount in a solution, for example sugar in sugar water.

Solution: A mixture of two or more substances that appears to be uniform throughout except on a molecular level.

Solvent: The major component of a solution or the liquid in which some other component is dissolved, for example water in sugar water.

Specific gravity: The ratio of the density of a substance to the density of another substance.

Spectrum: Range of individual wavelengths of radiation produced when white light is broken down into its component colors when it passes through a prism or is broken apart by some other means.

Standard: A base for comparison.

Star: A vast clump of hydrogen gas and dust that produces great energy through fusion reactions at its core.

Static electricity: A form of electricity produced by friction in which the electric charge does not flow in a current but stays in one place.

Streak: The color of the dust left when a mineral is rubbed across a surface.

Substrate: The substance on which an enzyme operates in a chemical reaction.

Succulent: Plants that live in dry environments and have water storage tissue.

Surface water: Water in lakes, rivers, ponds, and streams.

Suspension: A temporary mixture of a solid in a gas or liquid from which the solid will eventually settle out.

Symbiosis: A pattern in which two or more organisms live in close connection with each other, often to the benefit of both or all organisms.

Synthesis reaction: A chemical reaction in which two or more substances combine to form a new substance.

T

Taiga: A large land biome mostly dominated by coniferous trees.

Tectonic plates: Huge flat rocks that form Earth's crust.

Temperate: Mild or moderate weather conditions.

Temperature: The measure of the average energy of the molecules in a substance.

Terminal: A connection in an electric circuit; usually a connection on a source of electric energy such as a battery.

Terracing: A series of horizontal ridges made in a hillside to reduce erosion.

Testa: A tough outer layer that protects the embryo and endosperm of a seed from damage.

Thermal conductivity: A number representing a material's ability to conduct heat.

Thermal energy: Energy caused by the movement of molecules due to the transfer of heat.

Thiamine: A vitamin of the B complex that is essential to normal metabolism and nerve function.

Thigmotropism: The tendency for a plant to grow toward a surface it touches.

Titration: A procedure in which an acid and a base are slowly mixed to achieve a neutral substance.

Toxic: Poisonous.

Trace element: A chemical element present in minute quantities.

Translucent: Permits the passage of light.

Tropism: The growth or movement of a plant toward or away from a stimulus.

Troposphere: The lowest layer of Earth's atmosphere, ranging to an altitude of about 9 miles (15 km) above Earth's surface.

Tsunami: A tidal wave caused by an earthquake.

Tuber: An underground, starch-storing stem, such as a potato.

Tundra: A treeless, frozen biome with low-lying plants.

Turbulence: Air disturbance or unrest that affects an aircraft's flight.

Tyndall effect: The effect achieved when colloidal particles reflect a beam of light, making it visible when shined through such a mixture.

U

Ultraviolet: Electromagnetic radiation (energy) of a wavelength just shorter than the violet (shortest wavelength) end of the visible light spectrum and thus with higher energy than the visible light.

Unconfined aquifer: An aquifer under a layer of permeable rock and soil.

Unicellular: Living things that have one cell. Protozoans are unicellular.

Universal gravitation: The notion of the constancy of the force of gravity between two bodies.

V

Vacuole: A space-filling organelle of plant cells.

Variable: Something that can change the results of an experiment.

Vegetative propagation: A form of asexual reproduction in which plants are produced that are genetically identical to the parent.

Viable: The capability of developing or growing under favorable conditions.

Vibration: A regular, back-and-forth motion of molecules in the air.

Visible spectrum: Light waves visible to the eye.

Vitamin: A complex organic compound found naturally in plants and animals that the body needs in small amounts for normal growth and activity.

Volcano: A conical mountain or dome of lava, ash, and cinders that forms around a vent leading to molten rock deep within Earth.

Voltage: Also called potential difference; the amount of electric energy stored in a mass of electric charges compared to the energy stored in some other mass of charges.

Voltmeter: An instrument for measuring the conductivity or resistance in a circuit or the voltage produced by an electric source.

Volume: The amount of space occupied by a three-dimensional object; the amplitude or loudness of a sound.

W

Water (hydrologic) cycle: The constant movement of water molecules on Earth as they rise into the atmosphere as water vapor, condense into droplets and fall to land or bodies of water, evaporate, and rise again.

Waterline: The highest point to which water rises on the hull of a ship. The portion of the hull below the waterline is under water.

Water table: The upper surface of groundwater.

Water vapor: Water in its gaseous state.

Wave: A motion in which energy and momentum is carried away from some source.

Wavelength: The distance between the peak of a wave of light, heat, or energy and the next corresponding peak.

Weather: The state of the troposphere at a particular time and place.

Weather forecasting: The scientific predictions of future weather patterns.

Weight: The gravitational attraction of Earth on an object; the measure of the heaviness of an object.

Wetlands: Areas that are wet or covered with water for at least part of the year.

X

Xanthophyll: Yellow pigment in plants.

Xerophytes: Plants that require little water to survive.

Xylem: Plant tissue consisting of elongated, thick-walled cells that transport water and mineral nutrients.

experiment CENTRAL

chapter 13

Electricity

We know that electricity will flow through certain objects and not others. We are told that it is dangerous to plug in an ungrounded electrical device while standing in water because the electricity may flow through our bodies and the water to the ground, giving us a shock. But how, exactly, does water conduct electricity? Do all liquids conduct electricity equally well? And how have we made this property useful in our everyday lives?

How electricity flows through metals

Most of the electricity we use every day is conducted from its source through metal wires to the appliances we use. Most metals, such as copper, conduct electricity well because they possess a great number of free electrons. An **electron** is an extremely small particle with a single electrical charge that orbits the nucleus of an atom. Materials with few or no free electrons do not conduct electricity and are called **insulators.** They are commonly used to coat the wiring we use, allowing the electric current to flow safely and efficiently through the wire.

The flow of electrons in an electric current was the focus of many experiments done by the French scientist André-Marie Ampere (1775–1836). Ampere developed the system we now use for measuring this electron flow. The common electrical unit of measurement of current, the ampere or amp, is named for him.

How electricity flows through liquids

Electricity can flow through liquids by the process of **ionic conduction,** the movement of **ions** (charged particles) within the liquid.

experiment
CENTRAL

Words to Know

Amperage:
A measurement of current. The common unit of measure is the ampere or amp.

Circuit:
The complete path of an electric current including the source of electric energy.

Current:
The flow of electrical charge from one point to another.

Dry cell:
A source of electricity that uses a non-liquid electrolyte.

Words to Know

Electrode:
A material that will conduct an electrical current, usually a metal; used to carry electrons into or out of a battery.

Electrolyte:
Any substance that, when dissolved in water, conducts an electric current.

Substances that conduct electricity when they are dissolved in water are called **electrolytes.** When a positive **electrode** and a negative electrode (such as wires attached to the terminals of a battery) are placed in an electrolytic solution, ions transport free electrons between the two electrodes, bridging the gap and allowing the flow of electricity.

In the first experiment, you will determine whether certain substances are electrolytes. Using a **voltmeter,** you will test various solutions and liquids and compare them to find which conducts electricity the best. When the two **probes** (positive and negative) of the voltmeter are placed in a liquid, the meter will indicate how much current (from the battery inside the meter) is passing between the probes. A strong electrolyte will conduct more current, and a weak electrolyte will conduct less. Acids in water, such as lemon juice, make good electrolytes because they contribute many hydrogen ions. Other solutions, such as organic compounds that contain sugar and starch, contribute few or no hydrogen ions and do not conduct electricity well.

Electrolytes and ionic conduction make batteries work

The batteries used to power watches, flashlights, and cars all rely on electrolytes to function. The first battery was developed by the Italian scientist Alessandro Volta (1745–1827), who also invented

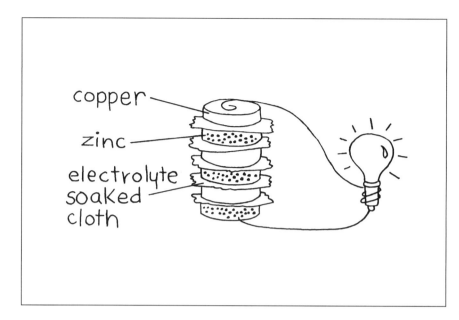

By combining different metals and a strong electrolyte, Alessandro Volta was able to create an electric current in a "Volta Pile," illustrated.

and gave his name to the measurement of the force of a current, called **voltage**. Volta discovered that a weak electric current is created when two different metals (he used copper and zinc) are pressed together, separated only by a thin layer of electrolyte-soaked fabric. The electrolyte between the metals carries free electrons from one to the other, creating an electric current. Combining a number of these "cells" in a series increases the force of the current, forming a useful battery.

Today's common household batteries, called **dry cell** batteries, use the same principle. One metal serves as a positive electrode, another metal serves as a negative electrode, and a dry electrolyte "paste" allows ionic conduction between the two. The batteries found in most cars are **wet cell** batteries, which use a liquid electrolyte to allow conduction.

In the second experiment, you will construct a single battery cell using two different metals and a lemon as an electrolyte. (Lemons contain citric acid.) After finding the voltage of that single cell, you will estimate how many lemons would be necessary in series to equal the voltage of a single D-cell battery. Finally, you will test your estimate and your hypothesis by constructing a multi-cell battery or "pile" and comparing its voltage to that of a D-cell battery.

Words to Know

Electron:
A subatomic particle that orbits the nucleus of an atom. It has a single electrical charge.

Hypothesis:
An idea in the form of a statement that can be tested by observation and/or experiment.

Ion:
An atom or groups of atoms that carry an electrical charge—either positive or negative—as the result of losing or gaining one or more electrons.

Ionic conduction:
The flow of an electrical current by the movement of charged particles, or ions.

Insulator:
A material through which little or no electrical current will flow.

Probe:
The terminal of a voltmeter, used to connect the voltmeter to a circuit.

Experiment 1
Electrolytes: Do some solutions conduct electricity better than others?

Purpose/Hypothesis

Using a voltmeter, we can determine how well different substances act as electrolytes by measuring their **resistance** when they are dissolved in water. The lower the resistance, the more conductive the electrolyte. In this experiment, you will predict whether certain substances are electrolytes. Before you begin, make an educated guess about the outcome of this experiment based on your knowledge of electricity and conductivity. This educated guess, or prediction, is your **hypothesis.** A hypothesis should explain these things:

- the topic of the experiment
- the variable you will change
- the variable you will measure
- what you expect to happen

A hypothesis should be brief, specific, and measurable. It must be something you can test through observation. Your experiment will prove or disprove whether your hypothesis is correct. Here is one possible hypothesis for this experiment: "Acids and other substances that

(W)ords to Know

Resistance:
A partial or complete limiting of the flow of electrical current through a material. The common unit of measure is the ohm.

Variable:
Something that can affect the results of an experiment.

Voltage:
Also called potential difference; a measurement of the amount of electric energy stored in a mass of electric charges compared to the energy stored in some other mass of charges. The common unit of measure is the volt.

Voltmeter:
An instrument for measuring the amperage, voltage, or resistance in an electrical circuit.

Wet cell:
A source of electricity that uses a liquid electrolyte.

What Are the Variables?

Variables are anything that might affect the results of an experiment. Here are the main variables in this experiment:

- the substances being tested for conductivity
- the concentration of the solutions
- the distance between the probes placed in the solutions

In other words, the variables in this experiment are everything that might affect conductivity. If you change more than one variable, you will not be able to tell which variable had the most effect on conductivity.

contribute hydrogen ions make better electrolytes than organic compounds such as sugars and starches."

In this case, the **variable** you will change is the material you use as an electrolyte, and the variable you will measure is the resistance of the solution. You expect acids, such as vinegar and lemon juice, will have lower resistance than sugars and starches and are therefore better electrolytes.

Level of Difficulty

Moderate.

Materials Needed

- 6 wide-mouth glass jars
- distilled water
- salt
- sugar
- cornstarch

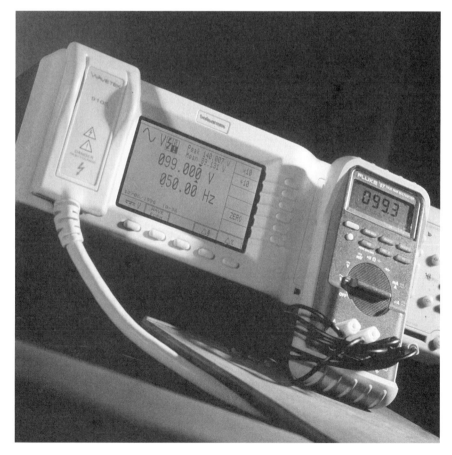

A voltmeter is used to measure the flow of current in a circuit. (Photo Researchers Inc. Reproduced by permission.)

- vinegar
- lemon juice
- adhesive labels or strips of masking tape
- voltmeter (most electronics supply stores carry these)
- measuring spoons
- stirrer

Approximate Budget
$30. (An inexpensive, analog voltmeter will suffice. Try to borrow one from school to reduce costs.)

Timetable
Less than 1 hour.

Step-by-Step Instructions
1. Pour 0.5 cup (0.125 liter) of distilled water in a jar. Add 1 table-spoon of salt and stir.

2. Label the jar with the name of the substance on an adhesive label or strip of masking tape.

3. Rinse your measuring spoon and stirrer thoroughly in distilled water and repeat steps 1 and 2, using the sugar in a second jar, and the cornstarch in a third jar.

4. Pour 0.5 cup (0.125 liter) of lemon juice into the fourth jar and 0.5 cup of vinegar into the fifth jar. The sixth jar will contain only

How to Experiment Safely
The battery in the voltmeter (usually one AA-cell) will provide all the voltage you will need for this experiment. Do not try to add batteries to the experiment, and NEVER experiment with household current or car batteries. Both are dangerous and potentially life-threatening.

If you choose to test other substances for conductivity, check with your science teacher to make sure you are not testing materials that will create a hazard (such as flammable liquids).

experiment
CENTRAL

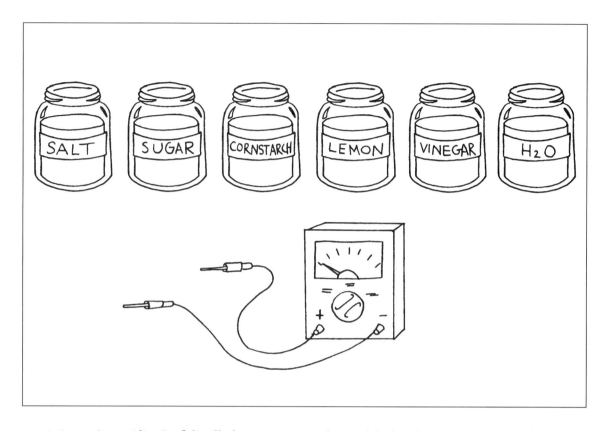

Steps 1 to 5: Electrolyte set-up.

0.5 cup (0.125 liter) of distilled water. Remember to label each jar, and rinse your measuring spoons and stirrers in distilled water after each mixture is prepared.

5. Place the glass jars so that the labels are visible. (Your set-up should look like the illustration.)

6. Set your voltmeter to measure resistance. Resistance is the measure of how much a circuit reduces the flow of electricity. With the probes touching, the voltmeter should read zero because there is no resistance, and all of the current is getting through. When you separate the probes, the meter goes to the other end of the scale and reads "infinity" because none of the current is getting through. To test something for measurable resistance, wet your fingertip and place the probes on it, just barely separated. The meter reading should shift slightly away from infinite resistance because a small current is flowing across your fingertip. If you are unsure how to set your voltmeter for resistance or which scale indicates resistance, check the meter's instruction manual.

Step 7: Probe tip set-up.

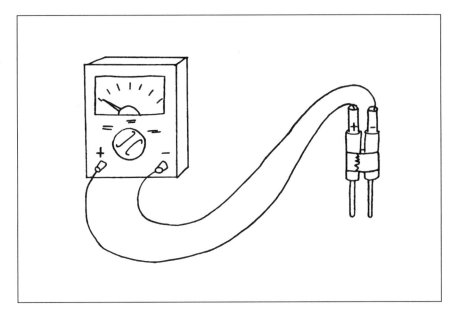

7. When testing the various substances, you must be sure that the voltmeter probes do not touch and that they remain at the same distance from each other for each test. (Otherwise you are adding another variable to your experiment.) Tape the probes together as illustrated. If necessary, place a ball of tape between the probe grips. Do not tape the metal part of the probes! The distance between the probe tips should be about 0.5 inch (1.25 centimeter).

8. Dip the electrodes into the first solution and observe the resistance reading on the voltmeter. Record your data, rinse the probes with distilled water, and repeat this step with each jar.

Summary of Results

Compare your data from the six different tests. Determine which of the substances are electrolytes and which are not. Rank them from strongest to weakest.

Check your findings against the predictions you made in your hypothesis. Which substances did you accurately predict would be electrolytes? Which substances did not behave as you expected?

Change the Variables

Think about the other variables you might change to investigate electrolytes. How would combining two electrolytes affect the results? Would lowering or raising the temperature of a solution affect con-

experiment
CENTRAL

Troubleshooter's Guide

This experiment requires careful attention when setting up your solutions and preparing the probes. Failing to wash a measuring spoon or allowing the probes to touch will alter your results. Here is a problem that may arise during the experiment, some possible causes, and some ways to remedy the problem:

Problem: The voltmeter is giving inconsistent readings or no readings.

Possible causes:

1. The voltmeter is not set properly to measure resistance. Check the instruction manual.

2. Your probe tips are too close to each other. Separate them and try again.

3. You have tape connecting the metal sections of the meter's probes.

4. The probe connections to the voltmeter are loose. Press the connections firmly into the voltmeter.

ductivity? Remember to check with your science teacher before heating or mixing substances. Does adding more of an electrolyte to a solution increase the conductivity? A number of interesting follow-up experiments can be performed using the same materials and methods.

Experiment 2

Batteries: Can a series of homemade electric cells form a "pile" strong enough to match the voltage of a D-cell battery?

Purpose/Hypothesis

In this experiment, you will construct a cell from copper and zinc electrodes and a lemon. The lemon contains citric acid, which is a weak electrolyte. After measuring the voltage of that one cell, you will add

What Are the Variables?

Variables are anything that might affect the results of an experiment. Here are the main variables in this experiment:

- the type of electrolyte used
- the metals used as electrodes
- the type and gauge (diameter) of wire used
- the number of cells placed in series

In other words, the variables in this experiment are everything that might affect the output voltage of your multiple-cell battery. If you change more than one variable, you will not be able to tell which variable had the most effect on the voltage.

more cells to the pile to attempt to match the voltage of a D-cell battery. Before you begin, make an educated guess about the outcome of this experiment based on your knowledge of batteries. This educated guess, or prediction, is your **hypothesis.** A hypothesis should explain these things:

- the topic of the experiment
- the variable you will change
- the variable you will measure
- what you expect to happen

A hypothesis should be brief, specific, and measurable. It must be something you can test through observation. Your experiment will prove or disprove whether your hypothesis is correct. Here is one possible hypothesis for this experiment: "A multicell battery constructed of zinc, copper, and lemons can equal the voltage output of a D-cell battery."

In this case, the **variable** you will change is the number of cells you place in series, and the variable you will measure is the output voltage. You expect that it is possible to equal the output voltage of a D-cell battery.

Level of Difficulty

Easy/moderate.

Materials Needed

- 10 lemons
- 10 copper nails (available at most hardware stores)
- 10 small zinc or zinc-plated nails or screws (available at most hardware stores)
- 10 feet (3 meters) of small diameter insulated copper wire
- fresh D-cell battery
- small flashlight bulb
- voltmeter with alligator-clip probes

Approximate Budget

$30. (An inexpensive analog voltmeter will suffice. Try to borrow one from school to reduce costs.)

Timetable

About 20 minutes.

Step-by-Step Instructions

1. Cut one 6-inch (15-centimeter) length of wire and strip the insulation off both ends.

2. Wind one end of the wire securely around a copper nail and push the copper nail into a lemon.

3. Cut a second 6-inch (15-centimeter) length of wire, strip the insulation off both ends, and wind one end around a zinc nail.

4. Push the zinc nail into the lemon about 1 inch (2.5 centimeters) from the copper nail. Be sure the two nails are not touching, either outside or inside the lemon, and avoid wetting the wire with lemon juice. Your cell should look like the illustration.

How to Experiment Safely

Do not change the number or type of battery used in this experiment without first consulting your science teacher. NEVER experiment with household current or car batteries! Both are dangerous and potentially life-threatening.

Step 4: A lemon cell.

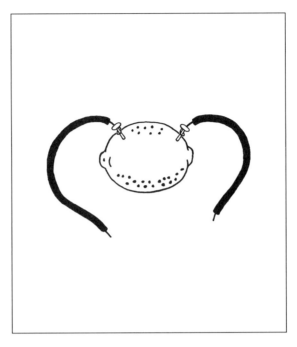

5. Set the voltmeter to measure direct current (DC) voltage. Connect the voltmeter to your cell by attaching one of the meter's alligator clips to each of the two loose wire ends. Observe and make note of the voltage of your cell.

6. Disconnect the voltmeter and use it to test the voltage of your D-cell battery by touching the probes to the positive and negative terminals of the cell. Make note of the voltage.

7. Calculate the minimum number of homemade lemon cells that would be needed to match the voltage of the D-cell battery. Do not be surprised if it is more lemons than you expected. That is one reason we do not power our flashlights with lemons!

8. Build as many lemon cells as needed and connect them in a series, as illustrated. Check the total voltage output of the "pile" after each lemon is added and make a note of the measurement on your data chart (see page 198). Remember the lemons must be connected properly, positive terminal (copper) to negative terminal (zinc). Your multicell battery should look something like the illustration.

9. After your battery is complete, test its voltage by touching the meter's probes to the loose wire ends. Because some current can be lost due to resistance in the wires and connections, you may need to add another lemon or two to match the D-cell's voltage. After your battery is powerful enough, connect the loose wire ends to the flashlight bulb—one wire to the bottom of the metal base and one to the side of the base. If your voltage reading is correct, it should light with the same intensity as when connected to the D-cell.

experiment
CENTRAL

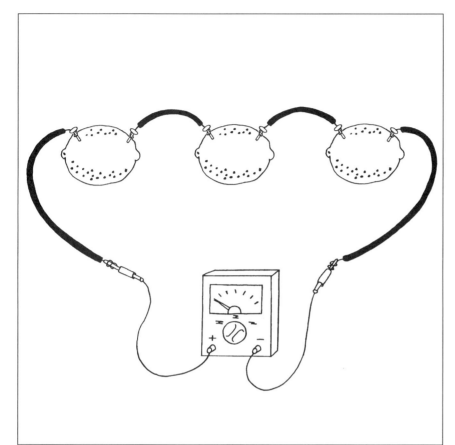

10. Examine your results and determine whether your hypothesis is true. If it is, you might connect both the lemon battery and the D-cell to flashlight bulbs to demonstrate the proof of your findings.

Summary of Results

Write a summary of your findings. Your data from Steps 8 and 9 should be recorded on a chart. This chart should contain the information that will show whether your hypothesis is correct. You can increase the clarity of your results by converting the data into graph form.

Change the Variables

Think about the other variables you might change to investigate other questions about electrolytes and batteries. Can you increase the output of a lemon cell by using different metals? Would lemon juice in a glass jar work more efficiently than an actual lemon? How much current could you produce with a Volta pile instead of a lemon cell? (A simple

experiment
CENTRAL

Voltage Chart

Number of lemons	Total voltage output	Powers flaslight?
1		
2		
3		
4		
5		
6		
7		
8		
9		
10		

Steps 8 and 9: Sample voltage chart.

Volta pile can be constructed using nickels, pennies, and an electrolyte-soaked paper towel.) After you know how to make a cell and measure its output, you can construct a number of interesting experiments comparing their output.

experiment
CENTRAL

Troubleshooter's Guide

This experiment involves a number of electrical connections that may need to be checked and rechecked to ensure that they are not loose. When you are doing experiments in electricity, the results can easily be affected by inexact assembly of your **circuit.** Many hobby stores carry some simple tools, such as battery holders, that will make experiments easier and more visually impressive. Here are some problems that may arise during your experiment, some possible causes, and some ways to remedy the problems:

Problem: The first lemon cell shows no voltage on the voltmeter.

Possible causes:

1. The voltmeter may be calibrated incorrectly. Check it by testing the D-cell. (Its voltage is printed on the battery case.)

2. The electrodes are placed too far apart or are touching. Remove and check the electrodes.

3. A connection is loose. Check all your connections and secure them with electrical tape if necessary.

Problem: The lemon cells connected together do not increase the total voltage as expected.

Possible causes:

1. Resistance in the wires is reducing voltage output. Shorten the length of the wires. Check that the bare wire ends are tightly wrapped around the nails.

2. The electrodes are placed too far apart or are inserted incorrectly. Check your electrodes.

3. Your hypothesis is incorrect. Your materials may not be sufficient to generate the voltage required. Consider what changes you could make to the electrodes and the electrolyte.

 **Design Your Own Experiment**

How to Select a Topic Relating to this Concept

Our everyday lives rely heavily upon batteries and electricity. Other aspects of this topic you might find valuable for exploration are rechargeable cells, photovoltaic cells, and the relationship between electrolytes and our bodies' functions.

Check the For More Information section and talk with your science teacher or school or community media specialist to start gathering information on electricity questions that interest you.

Steps in the Scientific Method

To do an original experiment, you need to plan carefully and think things through. Otherwise, you might not be sure what question you are answering, what you are or should be measuring, or what your findings prove or disprove.

Here are the steps in designing an experiment:

- State the purpose of—and the underlying question behind—the experiment you propose to do.
- Recognize the variables involved and select one that will help you answer the question at hand.
- State your hypothesis, an educated guess about the answer to your question.
- Decide how to change the variable you selected.
- Decide how to measure your results.

Recording Data and Summarizing the Results

In the experiments included here and in any experiments you develop, you can look for ways to make your data displays more accurate and interesting. For example, in the lemon experiment, try displaying the data from your chart in graph form.

Remember that those who view your results may not have seen the experiment performed, so you must present the information you have gathered in as clear a way as possible. Including photographs or illustrations of the steps in the experiment is a good way to show a viewer how you got from your hypothesis to your conclusion.

Related Projects

Simple variations on the two experiments in this section can prove valuable and informative. Some solids, for example, will act as electrolytes when melted. Find out which. Will an electrolytic solution work as efficiently when it is chilled in an ice bath? Figure out why or why not.

For More Information

McKeever, Susan, ed. *The DK Science Encyclopedia.* New York: DK Publishing, Inc., 1993. ❖ Contains informative entries on current, batteries, and circuits, as well as a number of good ideas for projects and demonstrations.

Ray, C. Claibourne. *The New York Times Book of Science Questions and Answers.* New York: Doubleday, 1997. ❖ Addresses both everyday observations and advanced scientific concepts on a wide variety of subjects.

chapter 14

Electromagnetism

Electromagnetism is the energy produced by an electric current moving through a metal core. To understand electromagnetism, you need to understand the basics of electricity.

What is electricity?

Electricity is produced by the movement of **electrons. Atoms** usually have a balanced or neutral electrical charge, with an equal number of electrons (with a negative charge) and **protons** (with a positive charge). However, some electrons can be removed from atoms, creating an imbalance. The atoms that lost electrons become positively charged, while the atoms that received electrons become negatively charged.

When the charge between two objects is unbalanced, the extra electrons on the negatively charged object are drawn toward the positively charged object in order to balance the charges again. This movement of electrons is electricity.

How can electricity create a magnet?

Objects with like charges (positive-positive or negative-negative) repel or push each other away, while objects with opposite charges (positive-negative) attract each other. A **magnetic field** can be produced by using electric charges to create attracting or repelling forces. For example, scientists discovered that when a wire is coiled around a piece of iron, and electric current flows through the wire, the iron becomes magnetized—an electromagnet.

Words to Know

Atom:
The smallest unit of an element, made up of protons and neutrons in a central nucleus surrounded by moving electrons.

Control experiment:
A set-up that is identical to the experiment but is not affected by the variable that will be changed during the experiment.

Electricity:
A form of energy caused by the presence of electrical charges in matter.

experiment
CENTRAL

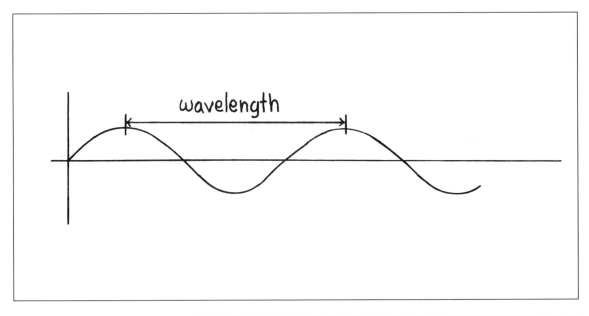

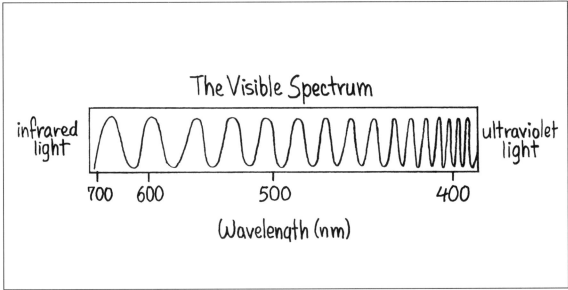

Electromagnetic waves are everywhere

When the force of a magnetic field alternates direction, first attracting and then repelling, it produces an electromagnetic **wave** that radiates away from the source. A wave of any kind can be described by two numbers: its wavelength and its frequency. The **wavelength** is the distance between the wave's highest points, or **peaks.** The **frequency** is the

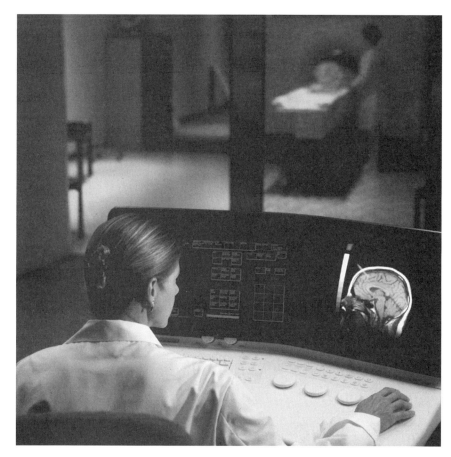

A magnetic resonance imaging (MRI) machine uses electricity and magnetism to create clear pictures of internal organs. (Photo Researchers Inc. Reproduced by permission.)

Words to Know

Electromagnetic spectrum:
The complete array of electromagnetic radiation, including radio waves (at the longest-wavelength end), microwaves, infrared radiation, visible light, ultraviolet radiation, X rays, and gamma rays (at the shortest-wavelength end).

Electron:
A subatomic particle with a single negative electrical change that orbits the nucleus of an atom.

Electromagnetism:
A form of magnetic energy produced by the flow of an electric current through a metal core.

Frequency:
The number of times a wave peak passes a given point every second.

Hypothesis:
An idea in the form of a statement that can be tested by observation and/or experiment.

number of those peaks that pass any point every second. Like other kinds of waves, electromagnetic waves carry energy at different frequencies, from very low (such as radio waves) to very high (such as gamma rays). X-rays, microwaves, and visible light are all kinds of electromagnetic **radiation.** The **electromagnetic spectrum** contains all these frequencies.

The study of electromagnetism is the study of the relationship between electricity and magnetism. The principles behind electromagnetism are used in electric motors and generators, televisions, diagnosis of illnesses, and in many other parts of our lives.

Exploring with magnets and electricity can be fascinating. Do you have questions about electromagnetism? You might be able to answer them by performing the following experiments.

Experiment 1
Magnetism: How can a magnetic field be created and detected?

Purpose/Hypothesis

In this experiment, you will demonstrate the relationship between electricity and magnetism and create and detect magnetic fields. Magnetic fields are all around us and are easy to create. Before you begin, make an educated guess about the outcome of this experiment based on your knowledge of electricity and magnetism. This educated guess, or prediction, is your **hypothesis.** A hypothesis should explain these things:

- the topic of the experiment
- the variable you will change
- the variable you will measure
- what you expect to happen

A hypothesis should be brief, specific, and measurable. It must be something you can test through observation. Your experiment will prove or disprove whether your hypothesis is correct. Here is one possible hypothesis for this experiment: "A magnetized needle will point perpendicularly through a charged wire, showing where the magnetic field produced by the wire lies."

(Words to Know

Magnet:
A material that attracts other like materials, especially metals.

Magnetic field:
An area around a magnet where magnetic forces act.

Peaks:
The points at which the energy in a wave is maximum.

Proton:
A subatomic particle with a single negative electrical change that is found in the nucleus of an atom.

Radiation:
Energy transmitted in the form of electromagnetic waves or subatomic particles.

Wave:
A means of transmitting energy in which the peak energy occurs at a regular interval.

What Are the Variables?

Variables are anything that might affect the results of an experiment. Here are the main variables in this experiment:

- the direction of the wire
- the magnetization of the needle
- the direction of the current

In other words, the variables in this experiment are everything that might affect the movement of the needle. If you change more than one variable, you will not be able to tell which variable had the most effect on the movement of the needle.

In this case, the **variable** you will change will be the magnetism of the needle, and the variable you will measure will be the movement of the needle. You expect the needle to be perpendicular to the wire.

Setting up a **control experiment** will help you isolate one variable. Only one variable will change between the control and the experimental condition, and that will be the magnetization of the needle. For the control, you will not magnetize the needle. Then you will be able to compare the movement of a magnetized and unmagnetized needle. If only the magnetized needle points perpendicular to the wire, your hypothesis will be supported.

Level of Difficulty
Moderate.

Materials Needed
- approximately 8 feet (2.4 meters) of 18- to 24-gauge insulated wire
- 2 metal sewing needles
- thread
- permanent magnet
- 6-volt lantern battery
- tape
- paper
- scissors

Approximate Budget
$20.

Timetable
Two hours.

Words to Know

Wavelength:
The distance between the peak of a wave of light, heat, or other form of energy and the next corresponding peak.

Variable:
Something that can affect the results of an experiment.

How to Experiment Safely

Any time you are experimenting with electricity, follow the directions exactly. The levels of electricity here are very low and cannot really hurt you, but electricity can always give you a shock if you are not extremely careful. Handle only wires covered with insulation, keep water away from the experiment, and keep your hands dry as you work. Do not use a vehicle battery. It is much too powerful and can cause a serious shock, or may even explode.

experiment
CENTRAL

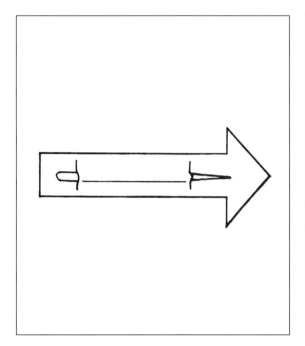

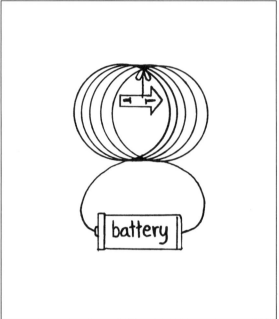

Step-by-Step Instructions

1. Magnetize the needle: Rub one side of the permanent magnet against the needle at least 30 times, always in the same direction.

2. Cut the paper into the shape of an arrow and stick the magnetized needle into the arrow lengthwise as illustrated.

3. Tape the thread to the top edge of the arrow.

4. Make a loop of wire about 3 inches (7.5 centimeters) in diameter. Continue to wrap the wire around this original loop, making a coil of five loops. Leave a length of wire free at either end.

5. Use the thread to tie the wire loops together tightly.

6. Then tie your paper arrow to the top of the loop. It should hang freely in the center of the loop.

7. Attach one end of the wire to each terminal of your battery—one to the positive terminal and one to the negative terminal.

8. Carefully observe the paper arrow.

9. Move the wire loop in different directions and watch what happens to the arrow.

Troubleshooter's Guide

Here is a problem that may arise during this experiment, some possible causes, and ways to remedy the problem.

Problem: The arrow is not affected when the wire loop is attached to the battery.

Possible causes:

1. The wires are not tightly connected to the battery. Check your connections and try again.

2. Your needle is not magnetized well enough. Pull it out of the arrow and rub your magnet across it a number of times. Be sure to rub it in only one direction with only one pole of the magnet.

3. You do not have enough loops of wire. Try looping some more wire around your original loop.

4. Your battery is dead. Replace it and try again.

10. Repeat the procedure with the other needle, but without magnetizing it. What do you observe?

Summary of Results

Record your observations. Where did the arrow point? What does that tell you about the location of the magnetic field produced by the electric current flowing through your wire loops? Was your hypothesis correct?

Change the Variables

You can vary this experiment in several ways. Try reversing the direction of the electric current by attaching the wires to the opposite terminals. Where does the arrow point now? You should find that the direction of the magnetic field depends on the direction of the electric current. You can also use different kinds of batteries with different voltages. See what effects they have on your magnetized needle, if any. Warning! Do not use a vehicle battery.

Experiment 2
Electromagnetism: How can an electromagnet be created?

Purpose/Hypothesis

Electric currents create magnetic fields. When you increase the strength of the current, you increase the strength of the magnetic field. In this experiment, you will demonstrate this by building an electromagnet and observing the movement of electric charges. Before you begin, make an educated guess about the outcome of this experiment based on your knowledge of electricity and magnetism. This educated guess, or prediction, is your **hypothesis.** A hypothesis should explain these things:

- the topic of the experiment
- the variable you will change
- the variable you will measure
- what you expect to happen

A hypothesis should be brief, specific, and measurable. It must be something you can test through observation. Your experiment will prove or disprove whether your hypothesis is correct. Here is one pos-

 ## What Are the Variables?

Variables are anything that might affect the results of an experiment. Here are the main variables in this experiment:

- the strength of the magnet

- the number of wire coils around nail

- the size of the nail

- the weight of the objects

In other words, the variables in this experiment are everything that might affect the number of objects that the electromagnet can pick up. If you change more than one variable, you will not be able to tell which variable had the most effect on the strength of the magnet.

sible hypothesis for this experiment: "The more wire you wrap around a nail attached to a battery, the stronger the nail's magnetism and the more objects it can pick up."

In this case, the **variable** you will change is the amount of wire wrapped around the nail, and the variable you will measure will be the number of objects it will pick up. You expect that by adding turns of wire you will be able to pick up more objects.

Only one variable will change between the **control experiment** and the experimental condition, and that is the number of wire coils around the nail. The control will have only one wire coil.

You will count how many paper clips your magnet is able to pick up as you add coils. If increasing the number of coils increases the number of objects it can pick up, your hypothesis was supported.

Level of Difficulty
Easy.

Materials Needed
- several feet (about 1 meter) of insulated wire
- 6-volt lantern battery
- large nail or bolt
- permanent magnet
- supply of metal paper clips

Approximate Budget
$20.

Timetable
2 hours to build and test.

 ## How to Experiment Safely
As with any project dealing with electricity, be extremely careful with wires and batteries. Keep everything away from water and keep your hands clean and dry. Do not use a vehicle battery. It is much too powerful and can cause a serious shock or may even explode.

Step-by-Step Instructions

1. As your control experiment, loop the wire loosely once around the nail.

2. Attach either end of the large wire loop to the battery's terminals.

3. Place a pile of paper clips on the table.

Step 1: Loop wire loosely once around the nail.

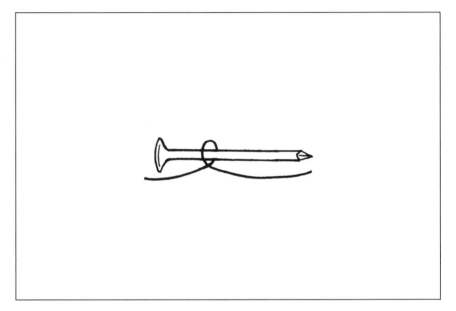

Step 4: Data sheet for Experiment 2.

Data Sheet

# of coils	# of clips picked up
0	—
1	—
2	—
3	—

4. Touch the nail to the paper clips. Record how many it picks up on a data sheet similar to the one illustrated.

5. Remove the nail and wire from the battery. Beginning at one end of the nail, wrap several tight loops around it, all in the same direction. Record the number of loops you wrap.

6. Again attach the end of the wire to the battery terminal. Touch the nail to the paper clips, and record how many stick to it.

7. Wrap more wire loops in the same direction. Attach the wire to the battery again and try picking up clips.

8. Repeat several times with more loops every time. Keep recording how many loops you wrap around the nail and how many clips it picks up.

Summary of Results

Study the results on your data sheet. Did more loops create a stronger magnetic field? How could you tell? Was your hypothesis correct? Summarize what you have discovered.

Troubleshooter's Guide

Below is a problem that may arise during this experiment, some possible causes, and ways to remedy the problem.

Problem: The electromagnet will not pick up any paper clips.

Possible causes:

1. The wire connections are not tight enough on the battery terminals. Check them and tighten.

2. You do not have enough loops around your nail. Try adding more in the same direction.

3. Your paper clips are too big for the strength of the magnet. Try using smaller paper clips or thumbtacks.

4. Your nail or bolt is dirty or not made of iron or steel. Try a different nail or bolt.

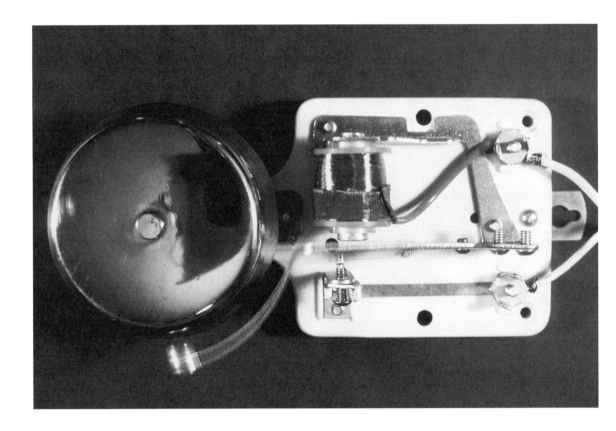

The electromagnet in this electric bell generates a current that activates the bell. (Peter Arnold Inc. Reproduced by permission.)

Change the Variables

You can vary this experiment. For example, try using a different kind of material for your magnet, such as wood or plastic. What happens? What can you conclude? Or try a much larger or smaller metal object as a magnet. What is the effect on the number of objects that the magnet can pick up?

You can also change the wire. Try thinner or thicker wire. What effect does that have on your magnetic field?

Try using different kinds of batteries, with smaller and larger voltages. What is your hypothesis about what will happen to the magnetic field? Warning! Do not use a vehicle battery.

Finally, you can experiment with different objects to pick up, smaller, larger, or made of different materials. What do you predict will happen?

experiment
CENTRAL

Design Your Own Experiment

How to Select a Topic Relating to this Concept

Are you interested in further exploring kinds of magnets, magnetic fields, and their relation to electric currents? Perhaps you would like to build your own electric motor, investigate static electricity, or explore how electromagnetism is used in generating electricity, computer memory, television images, and many other facets of electrical engineering.

Check the For More Information section and talk with your science teacher or school or community media specialist to start gathering information on electromagnetism questions that interest you.

Steps in the Scientific Method

To do an original experiment, you need to plan carefully and think things through. Otherwise you may not be sure what question you are answering, what you are or should be measuring, or what your findings prove or disprove.

Here are the steps in designing an experiment:

*   State the purpose of—and the underlying question behind—the experiment you propose to do.

We depend on electric motors, which depend on electromagnetism. (Peter Arnold Inc. Reproduced by permission.)

experiment
CENTRAL

- Recognize the variables involved, and select one that will help you answer the question at hand.
- State a testable hypothesis, an educated guess about the answer to your question.
- Decide how to change the variable you selected.
- Decide how to measure your results.

Recording Data and Summarizing the Results

Your data should include charts, such as the one you did for these experiments. They should be clearly labeled and easy to read. You may also want to include photos, graphs, or drawings of your experimental set-up and results.

If you are preparing an exhibit, display the devices you create to help explain what you did and what you discovered. Observers could even test your magnets. If you have done a nonexperimental project, explain clearly what your research question was and illustrate your findings.

Related Projects

In addition to experimental projects, you could build motors and large magnets that produce currents to light up a lamp or run an appliance. Or you could investigate the many uses of electromagnetism, especially the field of medicine. There are many possibilities!

For More Information

Whalley, Margaret. *Electricity and Magnetism.* Chicago: World Book, 1997. ❖ Introduces basic principles of electricity and magnetism through experiments and activities.

Wood, Robert, and Bill Wright. *Electricity and Magnetism Fundamentals: Funtastic Science Activities for Kids.* Philadelphia: Chelsea House Publishing, 1998. ❖ Through several different activities the relationship between electricity and magnetism is demonstrated.

Zubrowski, Bernie, and Ray Doty. *Blinkers and Buzzers: Building and Experimenting with Electricity and Magnetism.* New York: Beech Tree Books, 1991. ❖ Provides activities that use batteries, bulbs, and wire to create traffic lights, telegraphs, burglar alarms, and much more.

chapter 15

Enzymes

You could not run a race or digest food without **enzymes.** Actually, you could not grow up without enzymes working in your body. Present in all living things, enzymes are **catalysts,** that is, little chemical spark plugs that activate some 1,000 to 2,000 **reactions** in each cell. Enzymes control the way our bodies work. They help other life forms function as well. For example, the silkworm cannot break out of its cocoon without enzymes.

A hunk of meat, a hawk, and a discovery

Rene Antoine de Reaumur was a French scientist who wanted to know how food was digested. In 1750, he tried a unique experiment. Tying a very tiny metal cage containing a small piece of meat on a long string, he taught his pet hawk to swallow the cage. The string hung out of the bird's mouth, and de Reaumur very carefully pulled out the cage after fifteen minutes without injuring the animal. The meat did not look the same. Its color was gone and it looked puffy and soft. He tried the experiment two more times, leaving the cage inside longer. The meat was totally soft after one hour, and after three it looked like lumpy soup. De Reaumur did not know he had witnessed the work of enzymes, but his experiments gave other scientists the first clue about their existence and function.

What's in a name?

The word enzyme comes from two Greek words meaning "in yeast." German scientist Willy Kuhne came up with the term in 1876. Kuhne noticed that the yeast used to make bread acted as a catalyst, producing a chemical reaction. Once added to the dough in the bread-making

Words to Know

Catalase:
An enzyme found in animal liver tissue that breaks down hydrogen peroxide into oxygen and water.

Catalyst:
A compound that starts or speeds up the rate of a chemical reaction without undergoing any change in its own composition.

Control experiment:
A set-up that is identical to the experiment but is not affected by the variable that affects the experimental group.

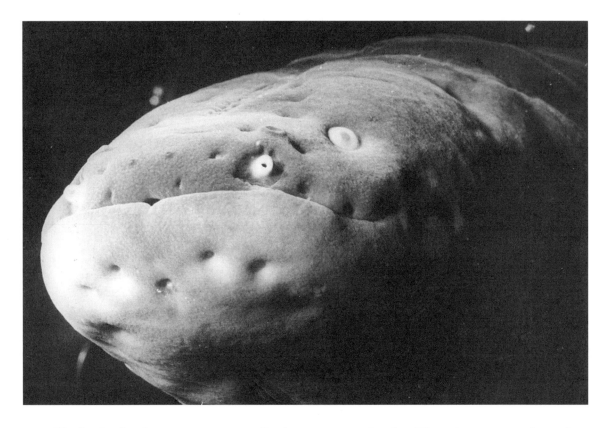

The electric eel needs enzymes to produce its electricity. (UPI/Corbis-Bettmann. Reproduced by permission.)

process, yeast splits into sugar molecules. They, in turn, produce alcohol and carbon dioxide. Carbon dioxide gas bubbles trapped in the dough cause it to rise. Kuhne reasoned that yeast was a catalyst for this new chemical compound, so he used the word enzyme to describe other catalysts.

Based on the work of de Reaumur and others, Kuhne understood that digestive juices were also catalysts, because they caused a reaction that broke food down into a simpler form. Catalyst is actually a Swedish word that means "to break down."

Pepsin was the first enzyme prepared from animal tissue. Extracted from the lining of the stomach, it aids digestion. Pepsin is actually a Greek word meaning "to digest." Later it was discovered that enzymes could work outside the living cell, which made them more useful to scientists.

As simple as a lock and key

There are up to 100,000 different enzymes in one cell. Each enzyme is responsible for a single reaction within the cell, and the process works

Yeast is the catalyst that caused this bread to rise. (Corbis Corp. Reproduced by permission.)

like a lock and key. As the key, each enzyme has a specific shape. It targets a specific **substrate,** the substance on which the enzyme does its work. This substrate, which matches the shape and size of the enzyme, is the lock. Each enzyme can only work with one substrate or, at most, a small number of chemically related substrates. After the substrate and enzyme come together, a new compound is activated and formed. The study of how an enzyme behaves is called **enzymology.**

Enzyme industry

By-products of animals slaughtered for meat provide animal enzymes, but no animal is raised just for enzymes. **Rennin,** an enzyme in the stomach lining of slaughtered calves, is used to make cheese. Plants provide other enzymes. Papain, an enzyme from the fruit of the papaya tree, helps digestion. It also tenderizes meat and is used as an antibacterial cleaner for bad wounds. Enzymes are also chemically produced in factories.

Remember the yeast Kuhne observed? Yeast has an enzyme that not only helps to make bread but also activates the process of making beer and wine. The yeast is grown in large tanks. When it starts producing enzymes, they are removed. Other enzymes produced by bacteria are used in some laundry products to help break down stains.

Life processes cannot function without enzymes. Conducting experiments will help you become familiar with these important chemicals.

Experiment 1
Finding the Enzyme: Which enzyme breaks down hydrogen peroxide?

Purpose/Hypothesis

Without enzymes, many chemical reactions do not take place. In this experiment you will identify the presence of an enzyme in liver tissue, known as **catalase,** that breaks down highly reactive hydrogen peroxide into harmless water and oxygen. This is an important chemical reaction that takes place inside the body. Catalase prevents the potentially destructive oxidation effects of any hydrogen peroxide that may be generated in the body as the result of various other chemical reactions.

To begin this experiment, use what you know about enzymes to make an educated guess about how the enzymes in liver tissue will affect hydrogen peroxide. This educated guess, or prediction, is your **hypothesis.** A hypothesis should explain these things:

What Are the Variables?

Variables are anything that might affect the results of an experiment. Here are the main variables in this experiment:

- Tissue freshness—use only fresh, raw materials, nothing cooked or frozen.

- Tissue temperature—all materials should be at room temperature.

- Tissue quantity—this experiment will tell you how much plant and animal tissue is to be used and how to process it.

In other words, the variables in this experiment are everything that might affect the chemical reaction of the materials with the hydrogen peroxide. If you change more than one variable, you will not be able to tell which variable had the most effect on the chemical reaction. Alterations may change the rate of the reaction or result in the **denaturization** of the enzymes.

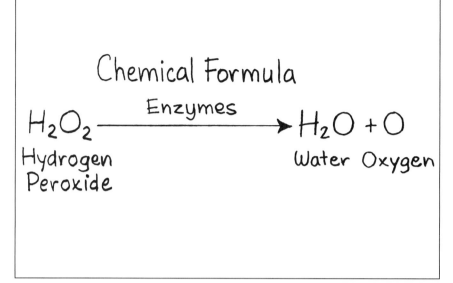

Chemical Formula

$$H_2O_2 \xrightarrow{\text{Enzymes}} H_2O + O$$

Hydrogen Peroxide

Water Oxygen

Chemical formula showing hydrogen peroxide broken down by enzymes into water and oxygen.

- the topic of the experiment
- the **variable** you will change
- the variable you will measure
- what you expect to happen

A hypothesis should be brief, specific, and measurable. It must be something you can test through observation. Your experiment will prove or disprove whether your hypothesis is correct. Here is one possible hypothesis for this experiment: "Animal liver tissue contains the enzyme that breaks down hydrogen peroxide."

In this case, the variable you will change is the material being tested, liver in one cup and potato in another cup, and the variable you will measure is the presence of oxygen bubbles. Your cup filled with water will serve as a **control experiment** to allow you to observe any oxygen bubbles that might be produced without the presence of hydrogen peroxide. If the liver sample reacts with hydrogen peroxide and produces oxygen bubbles and the water sample does not, you will know your hypothesis is correct.

Level of Difficulty
Easy/moderate.

Materials Needed
- 1 small piece of liver—fresh, never frozen or cooked
- 1 potato—fresh, never frozen or cooked

- hydrogen peroxide
- 4 clear cups—plastic or glass
- knife
- spoon or lab spatula
- water
- goggles
- labels

Approximate Budget
Less than $10 for hydrogen peroxide, potato, and liver.

Timetable
Approximately 20 minutes.

Step-by-Step Instructions
1. Cut a 0.5-inch (1.25-centimeter) cube of liver and smash it into a paste using a spoon. Place it in a cup.

2. Smash another 0.5-inch (1.25-centimeter) cube of liver into a paste. Place it into a separate cup. (Don't forget to clean the spoon.)

3. Cut a 0.5-inch (1.25-centimeter) cube of potato and smash it. Place it in a separate cup.

4. Smash another 0.5-inch (1.25-centimeter) cube of potato and place it in the last cup.

5. Label the cups:
   Cup 1: Liver and water
   Cup 2: Liver and hydrogen peroxide
   Cup 3: Potato and water
   Cup 4: Potato and hydrogen peroxide

How to Experiment Safely
Wear goggles when handling hydrogen peroxide. If you accidentally get some on your skin, wash it off quickly. Also be careful not to get it near your eyes, ears, nose, or mouth. You will be handling raw meat, so you must carefully wash all surfaces before and after the experiment. Do not eat the meat after the experiment.

Steps 5 to 7: Set-up of control and test cups.

6. Fill cups 1 and 3 halfway with water. These will serve as your control experiment.

7. Fill cups 2 and 4 halfway with hydrogen peroxide. These will test which material has the enzyme.

8. Observe what takes place. If the enzyme for the breakdown of hydrogen peroxide is present, oxygen will form bubbles. When hydrogen peroxide breaks down, it separates into water and oxygen.

9. Record your results.

Troubleshooter's Guide

Here is a problem that may arise during this experiment, a possible cause, and a way to remedy the problem.

Problem: Nothing happened in any of the cups.

Possible cause: The materials may be too old. Check the freshness of the tissue samples as well as of the hydrogen peroxide. Hydrogen peroxide needs to be stored in a dark bottle and capped at all times.

	with water	with hydrogen peroxide
Liver		
Potato		

Summary of Results

Make a chart like the one illustrated to show what you observed. Determine which tissue has the enzymes that cause the breakdown of the hydrogen peroxide into water and oxygen. Was it the tissue you predicted in your hypothesis?

Change the Variables

You can change the variables and conduct a similar experiment. For example, place the pieces of liver and potato in the refrigerator to see if temperature affects the action of the enzyme.

Experiment 2
Tough and Tender: Does papain speed up the aging process?

Purpose/Hypothesis

This experiment deals with the aging process of beef. The older or more aged meat is, the softer the meat tends to be. This is a natural process of **decomposition**, the breakdown of organic matter. Beef can take weeks to become tender, but a natural tenderizer called papain can speed up the process. Papain is an enzyme extracted from the papaya fruit.

experiment
CENTRAL

What Are the Variables?

Variables are anything that might affect the results of an experiment. Here are the main variables in this experiment:

- the kind of meat—only beef from a steak or filet should be used.

- the type of tenderizer or enzyme—use the natural tenderizer extracted from the papaya fruit.

- the amount of tenderizer used.

- the temperature—the control and experimental meat must both be aged in the refrigerator.

- the amount of time the tenderizer is in place on the beef.

In other words, the variables in this experiment are everything that might affect the degree of decomposition of the beef. If you change more than one variable, you will not be able to tell which variable had the most effect on the decomposition process.

To begin the experiment, use what you know about enzymes to make an educated guess about how papain will affect the aging process of beef. This educated guess, or prediction, is your **hypothesis.** A hypothesis should explain these things:

- the topic of the experiment
- the **variable** you will change
- the variable you will measure
- what you expect to happen

A hypothesis should be brief, specific, and measurable. It must be something you can test through observation. Your experiment will prove or disprove whether you hypothesis is correct. Here is one possible hypothesis for this experiment: "Beef will age faster if it is sprinkled with papain."

In this case, the variable you will change is whether papain tenderizer is used on the beef, and the variable you will measure is the appearance of the meat after 24 hours. If the meat with the tenderizer is more decomposed, you will know your hypothesis is correct.

Level of Difficulty
Easy/moderate.

Materials Needed
- beef from a steak or filet—8 to 10 ounces (230 to 250 grams) is sufficient
- Adolph's All Natural Tenderizer, a natural tenderizer made from papaya
- 2 plastic storage containers with lids
- measuring spoons
- toothpicks
- slides
- microscope
- stain (optional—congo red or methalene blue)

Note: Do not add any additional solutions to the meat. For example, vinegar may stop the enzyme process.

Approximate Budget
About $15. (Price of beef will vary. You can borrow a microscope from a friend or use one in school.)

Timetable
About 24 hours—10 minutes to set up the experiment and 30 minutes to view the results; the rest is storage time in the refrigerator.

Step-By-Step Instructions
1. In two plastic containers, place equal amounts of beef steak.

2. Sprinkle about 1/2 teaspoon of meat tenderizer on one steak.

How to Experiment Safely

In this experiment you will handle raw meat, so you must carefully wash all surfaces before and after the experiment. Do not eat the meat after the experiment. Be careful not to get meat tenderizer in your eyes.

experiment
CENTRAL

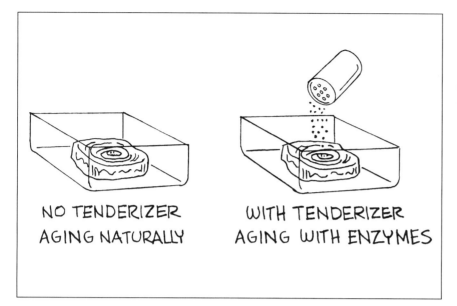

NO TENDERIZER
AGING NATURALLY

WITH TENDERIZER
AGING WITH ENZYMES

Step 2: Sprinkle about 1/2 teaspoon of meat tenderizer on one steak, leaving the other to age naturally.

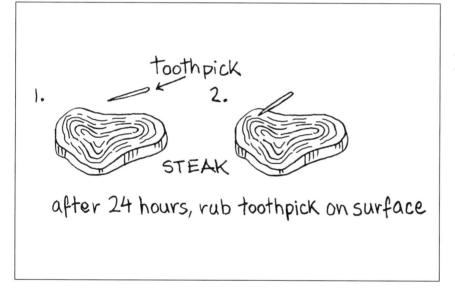

1.

toothpick

2.

STEAK

after 24 hours, rub toothpick on surface

Step 5: After the storage period, use a clean toothpick to scratch the surface of the meat without the tenderizer.

3. Seal both containers and mark the lid of the container with the tenderized steak "Tenderizer."

4. Place both containers in the refrigerator and leave for 24 hours.

5. After the storage period, use a clean toothpick to scratch the surface of the meat without the tenderizer.

6. Wipe the toothpick onto a clean slide. (Add one drop of stain if you wish.)

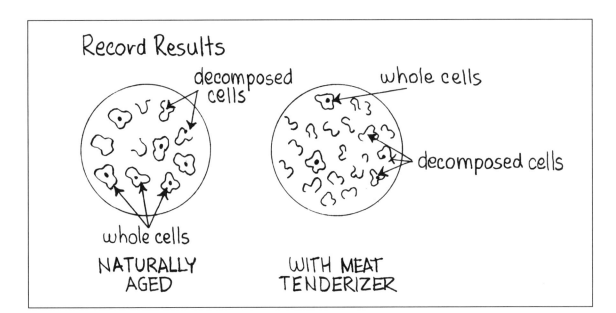

Record Results

decomposed cells

whole cells

whole cells

NATURALLY AGED

decomposed cells

WITH MEAT TENDERIZER

Step 7: Slide views of naturally aged and tenderized meat cells.

7. View the slide under the microscope at 40 to 70 medium power. Record your results.

8. Repeat Steps 5 to 7 for the piece of meat with the tenderizer.

Summary of Results

Reflect on your hypothesis. The goal was to cause an increase in decomposition of meat (speed up the aging process to make the meat tender). Was your hypothesis correct? This should be evident in large

Troubleshooter's Guide

Here is a problem that may arise during this experiment, a possible cause, and a way to remedy the problem.

Problem: You cannot see a difference in decomposition.

Possible cause: Decomposition is not obvious at this point. Stain the cells. Cells that have not experienced decomposition have a nuclei inside. When decomposition takes place, the cell membrane is broken and the nucleus is released.

amounts of decayed cells. Is it true? Did more cells decay with tenderized meat? Write a summary of your findings.

Change the Variables

You can change the variables and conduct similar experiments. For example, you can vary the amount of tenderizer used to see if that changes the degree of decomposition. You can also change the amount of time for the experiment to 36 or 48 hours.

 # Design Your Own Experiment

How to Select A Topic Relating to this Concept

Enzymes and the chemical reactions they produce are all around you. If you can identify one reaction, you have a start. Once you discover a chemical reaction, find out what is taking place. For example, the solid food you eat is turned into other substances by enzymes. What exactly are those enzymes? What do they do?

Check the For More Information section and talk with your science teacher or school or community media specialist to start gathering information on enzyme questions that interest you. As you consider possible experiments, be sure to discuss them with your science teacher or another knowledgeable adult before trying them. Some of the materials or processes might be dangerous.

Steps in the Scientific Method

To do an original experiment, you need to plan carefully and think things through. Otherwise, you might not be sure what question you are answering, what you are or should be measuring, or what your findings prove or disprove.

Here are the steps in designing an experiment:

*   State the purpose of—and the underlying question behind—the experiment you propose to do.
*   Recognize the variables involved, and select one that will help you answer the question at hand.
*   State a testable hypothesis, an educated guess about the answer to your question.

- Decide how to change the variable you selected.
- Decide how to measure your results.

Recording Data and Summarizing the Results

Photos, illustrations, and graphs are great visuals. Make clear the beginning question, the variable you changed, the variable you measured, the results, and your conclusion. Label everything clearly and show how it fits together.

Related Projects

Try changing the conditions of the enzyme reactions. For example, add vinegar to the hydrogen peroxide. Or cook the liver and potato before testing.

For More Information

The Dorling Kindersley Science Encyclopedia. New York: Dorling Kindersley, Inc., 1993. ❖ Contains several well-illustrated chapters such as "Catalysts," "Digestion," and "Chemistry of the Body" that discuss enzymes.

Lopez, D. A. *Enzymes: The Fountain of Life.* Neville Press, 1994. ❖ Provides examples of how enzymes make our bodies work.

chapter 16

Erosion

Soil **erosion** is the process by which **topsoil** is carried away by water, wind, or ice. Different types of soil have different abilities to absorb water, and so, are affected by erosion in varying degrees. Bare soil and soil on steep slopes are especially vulnerable to erosion.

Is erosion a new problem?

Throughout history, people have been affected by soil erosion due to natural conditions, as well as erosion caused by their own actions. As long ago as 4500 B.C., the Sumerians cleared land to grow food. They irrigated the land by building canals in the fertile valley where the Tigris and Euphrates rivers meet (in present-day Iraq). During the time of the Babylonian culture, which followed the Sumerians in about 1800 B.C., the people continued to dig canals. The rivers became muddy, and deposits of **silt,** medium-sized soil particles, settled in the irrigation canals and clogged them. The people had to carry silt out of the canals in baskets to keep the water flowing.

Over time, the people began to neglect the canals. As silt filled the valley, the land could support fewer and fewer people. About 700 years ago, the Babylonian canals were finally destroyed by the invasion of the Mongols, and the land returned to desert.

Is erosion a problem in the United States?

Not long ago, in the 1930s, North American prairies suffered from extreme wind erosion. During a period of high rainfall, large expanses of land were plowed to grow wheat. This period was followed by

Words to Know

Control experiment:
A set-up that is identical to the experiment but is not affected by the variable that affects the experimental group. Results from the control experiment are compared to results from the actual experiment.

Drought:
A prolonged period of dry weather that damages crops or prevents their growth.

Ecosystem:
An ecological community, including plants, animals, and microorganisms, considered together with their environment.

During the Dust Bowl, winds blew away as much as 3 to 4 inches (8 to 10 centimeters) of topsoil, ruining farmland. (Photo Researchers Inc. Reproduced by permission.)

years of **drought.** The exposed soil of the fields was blown away in hot, dry wind storms. The blowing soil of the Dust Bowl, as it was called, blackened the skies, ruined crops, and left farm fields bare and unproductive.

Today we often hear about erosion. Satellite images show red earth spilling into the ocean off the coast of the island of Madagascar. Here, and in many other places where people clear tropical forests and grow crops on hillsides, extremely high rates of erosion carry away massive quantities of topsoil.

It is important to understand why erosion occurs and how humans both cause it and are affected by it. Erosion is something that concerns everyone. Erosion affects the places where we live and our sources of food and water. It also affects our recreation areas—trails, beaches, lakes, and rivers.

What kind of questions do you have about erosion? You'll have an opportunity to explore the erosion process in the following experiments. You will also think about designing your own experiments to

Words to Know

Erosion:
The process by which topsoil is carried away by water, wind, or ice action.

Hypothesis:
An idea in the form of a statement that can be tested by observation and/or experiment.

experiment
CENTRAL

learn more about this natural phenomenon and how it can have a huge impact on our lives.

On hillsides that no longer have tree roots to hold topsoil in place, rain easily carries the soil into the ocean. (Liaison Agency. Reproduced by permission.)

Experiment 1
Erosion: Does soil type affect the amount of water that runs off a hillside?

Purpose/Hypothesis

In this experiment, you will find out how the type of soil affects how much erosion can occur. Soil is a mixture of **inorganic** materials (rocks, sand, silt, or clay) and **organic** materials (decomposing leaves and organisms). The ratio of these components to each other determines the kind of soil and its texture. In turn, the texture of soil determines how well the soil can support plants and withstand erosion.

ⓦ**ords to Know**

Inorganic:
Not made of or coming from living things.

Organic:
Made of or coming from living things.

experiment
CENTRAL

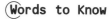

Before you begin, make an educated guess about the outcome of this experiment based on your knowledge of soils and erosion. This educated guess, or prediction, is your **hypothesis.** A hypothesis should explain these things:

- the topic of the experiment
- the variable you will change
- the variable you will measure
- what you expect to happen

A hypothesis should be brief, specific, and measurable. It must be something you can test through observation. Your experiment will prove or disprove your hypothesis. Here is one possible hypothesis for this experiment: "The looser and coarser the texture of the soil, the less runoff and erosion will occur."

In this case, the **variable** you will change will be the texture of the soil, and the variables you will measure are the amount of water that runs off and the amount of soil it carries with it, judged by the color of the runoff water. You expect the looser and coarser soils to have less water runoff and less soil erosion.

Setting up a **control experiment** will help you isolate one variable. Only one variable will change between the control and the experimental soil pans, and that variable is the kind of soil used. For the con-

What Are the Variables?

Variables are anything that might affect the results of an experiment. Here are the main variables in this experiment:

- the kind of soil used
- the slope of the soil
- the rate at which you pour water on the slope

In other words, the variables in this experiment are everything that might affect the amount of water and soil that run off. If you change more than one variable, you will not be able to tell which variable had the most effect on the runoff and erosion.

trol, you will use potting soil. For your experimental soil pans, you will use sand, clay, and neighborhood soil.

You will measure the amount of water that runs off your soil pans and how much erosion occurs. If the looser- and coarser-textured soils have less runoff, your hypothesis is correct.

Level of Difficulty

Moderate, because of materials needed.

Materials Needed

- 2 to 3 pounds (1 to 1.5 kilograms) of purchased potting soil
- 2 to 3 pounds (1 to 1.5 kilograms) sand
- 2 to 3 pounds (1 to 1.5 kilograms) clay
- 2 to 3 pounds (1 to 1.5 kilograms) neighborhood soil
- 4 shallow pans. Cookie sheets with 0.5 to 1.0 inch (1.25 to 2.5 centimeters) high edges work well.
- 4 glass jars, approximately 24 fluid ounces (680 milliliters)
- scrap lumber
- a sprinkler can or hose nozzle with mist setting
- water
- measuring cup
- labels
- outdoor area to conduct experiment, since it may be messy
- a baking dish, approximately 9 x 13 x 2 inches (23 x 33 x 5 centimeters)
- magnifying glass (optional)

Approximate Budget

$10 if soils must be purchased.

Timetable

2 to 3 hours.

 ## How to Experiment Safely

Wash your hands carefully after you handle soil, especially if you are using soil from outdoors. Be careful when digging to avoid broken glass or other trash in the soil.

Step-by-Step Instructions

1. First, examine your soils. You may want to look at their particles with a magnifying glass. On your chart (see illustration) record your soils in the order of their textures, from coarse to fine. If you cannot see separate particles, then the texture is very fine.

2. Place your shallow pans in a row and place a different kind of soil in each one. Fill each pan evenly up to its edges all around.

Steps 3 to 6: Set-up of soil "hillside."

Steps 8 to 10: Labeled jars containing different types of soil run-off.

3. Prop one end of your potting soil pan on a board to simulate a hill. The exact slope is not important, but you must use the same slope for each pan.

4. Place the bottom end of the pan so it is resting in the baking dish.

5. Measure 3 cups of water into your sprinkler can.

6. Sprinkle the water over your "hillside," mostly from the top edge, and watch what happens.

7. After the can is empty, wait 5 minutes.

8. Pour the water from the baking dish pan into a glass jar. Look at its color and measure how much you have collected. The darker the water, the more soil has run off.

9. Label the jar with the type of soil.

10. Repeat the procedure for sand, clay, and neighborhood soil.

Summary of Results
Record your results on a chart like the one illustrated.

Recording chart for Experiment 1.

Soil type	Amount of water used	Amount of water collected	Water color
1.			
2.			
3.			
4.			

Troubleshooter's Guide

Experiments do not always work out as planned. Even so, figuring out what went wrong can definitely be a learning experience. Here are some problems that may arise during this experiment, some possible causes, and some ways to remedy the problems.

Problem: Soil is sliding down the pans.

Possible cause: The incline of your pans is too steep. Try lowering the support on which you are resting your pans.

Problem: No water is running off.

Possible cause: You are not using enough water for the amounts and kinds of soil you are using. Use more water, but be sure you use the same amount for all of your trials.

Problem: All the runoff water is clear.

Possible cause: Your soils are packed very tightly so no soil comes off with the water. Try stirring your soils a bit in their pans. But remember, even if the water is clear, it could still be carrying away nutrients instead of bringing those nutrients to plants that need them.

Compare the amounts and colors of water in each jar. The darker the water, the more soil has run off in it. What have you discovered? Did coarser soils have less runoff? Was your hypothesis correct? Fill in your chart carefully and summarize what you found.

Change the Variables

You can vary this experiment by changing the variables. For example, use soils from different areas of your neighborhood (near a stream, a park, a baseball diamond) or buy different kinds of potting soils from a plant-supply store. Or try mixing your soils. Just record how much of each kind you use in each mixture. You can also try propping up your plants at different slopes, such as 30 degrees, 45 degrees, 60 degrees, and so on. Using the same kind of soil and different slopes, run several more trials. What happens? How does slope affect erosion?

experiment
CENTRAL

Experiment 2
Plants and Erosion: How do plants affect the rate of soil erosion?

Purpose/Hypothesis

Soil is an important part of an ecosystem. An **ecosystem** is a community of plants, animals, and microorganisms considered together with their environment. Because soil is the foundation for life on Earth, erosion can be a serious problem for the living beings that depend upon it—including humans.

In this experiment, you will explore how the rate of soil erosion is affected by plants growing on the soil. Plant cover—either growing plants or fallen leaves and branches—protects soil from erosion by slowing down flowing water or absorbing the impact of rain drops. Roots of trees and other plants help to prevent erosion by holding the soil in place. Roots absorb water and provide stability to the soil. Before you begin, make an educated guess about the outcome of this experiment based on your knowledge of soils, plants, and erosion. This educated guess, or prediction, is your **hypothesis**. A hypothesis should explain these things:

*   the topic of the experiment
*   the variable you will change

What Are the Variables?

Variables are anything that might affect the results of an experiment. Here are the main variables in this experiment:

*   the kind of soil used

*   the slope of the soil

*   the rate at which you pour water on the slope

   In other words, the variables in this experiment are everything that might affect the amount of water and soil that run off. If you change more than one variable, you will not be able to tell which variable had the most effect on the runoff and erosion.

Many organisms live in the soil and are threatened by erosion. (Photo Researchers Inc. Reproduced by permission.)

- the variable you will measure
- what you expect to happen

A hypothesis should be brief, specific, and measurable. It must be something you can test through observation. Your experiment will prove or disprove whether your hypothesis is correct. Here is one possible hypothesis for this experiment: "Less soil will erode from a hillside with plant cover (a layer of leaves or growing grass) than from a hillside with no plant cover."

experiment
CENTRAL

In this case, the **variable** you will change is the amount of plant cover, and the variables you will measure are the amount of water that runs off and the color of the soil that runs off. You expect the looser and coarser soils to have less water runoff and soil erosion.

Setting up a **control experiment** will help you isolate one variable. Only one variable will change between the control and the experimental trays, and that variable is the presence or absence of growing plants or plant cover. For the control, you will use potting soil without any vegetation. For your experimental trays, you will use grass and leaf litter (leaves and/or grass clippings).

You will measure how much erosion occurs in each of the trays by measuring water that runs off and comparing the color of the water. If the experimental trays show less erosion than the control tray, then your hypothesis was correct.

Level of Difficulty

Moderate, because of materials and time required.

Materials Needed

- 2 to 3 pounds (1 to 1.5 kilograms) purchased potting soil
- 1 to 2 pounds (0.5 to 1.0 kilograms) small gravel
- leaf litter (fallen leaves, twigs, and grass clippings)
- grass seed
- 3 shallow pans or trays (plant trays from a garden shop are designed to allow drainage; you may wish to use glass casserole dishes that allow you to observe the roots; otherwise, cookie sheets with edges will work.)
- 4 glass jars, approximately 24 fluid ounces (680 milliliters)
- a sprinkler can or hose nozzle with mist setting
- water
- labels
- measuring cup
- board or scrap lumber
- an area with adequate light for growing grass
- an outside area or other place for conducting the experiment, which may be messy
- a baking dish, approximately 9 x 13 x 2 inches (23 x 33 x 5 centimeters) or a dish pan to collect water that runs off

experiment
CENTRAL

Approximate Budget

$10 if soil and plant trays are purchased.

Timetable

Approximately 2 weeks.

Step-by-Step Instructions

1. Prepare three trays by putting an equal amount of potting soil in each tray. If you are using pans or cookie sheets, spread a layer of gravel on the bottom of the pan before adding the soil. This will allow for drainage since you will be watering all three pans while the grass is growing.

2. Set Tray 1 aside. In Tray 2, cover the soil with a layer of leaves and grass clippings. In Tray 3, sprinkle grass seed on the top of the soil.

3. Place the three trays in a place where they are level and have similar light and temperature conditions. (The temperature must be above 50°F (10°C) for the grass to grow.)

Step 2: Set-up of Tray 1, Tray 2, and Tray 3 and their contents.

4. Use the sprinkling can to give each tray the same amount of water. Continue watering all three trays approximately every 3 days until the grass in Tray 3 is about .5 inches (1.25 centimeters) tall. This may take one week or longer. You may have to adjust your water-

Tray 1
Soil

Tray 2
Leaf Litter

Tray 3
Grass Seed

experiment
CENTRAL

ing schedule depending on how fast the soil dries. Check the soil daily to see if it looks and feels moist.

5. When the grass has grown, you are ready to do the erosion test. Prop the end of Tray 1 (soil only) on a board to simulate a hill. The exact slope is not important, but you must use the same slope for each tray.

6. Place the bottom end of the tray so it is resting in the baking dish or dish pan.

7. Measure 3 cups of water into the sprinkler can.

8. Sprinkle the water over your "hillside," mostly from the top edge, and watch what happens.

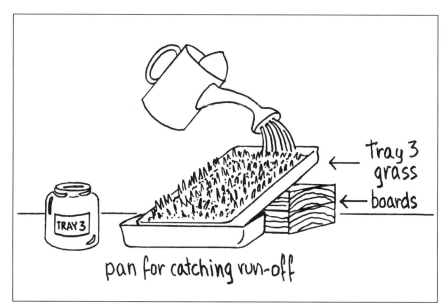

Steps 5 to 8: Set-up of erosion "hillside."

9. When the can is empty, wait 5 minutes.

10. Pour the water from the baking pan into a glass jar. Look at its color and measure how much you have collected.

11. Label your jar (Tray 1: soil only).

12. Repeat procedure for Tray 2 (soil with leaf litter) and Tray 3 (soil with grass). Be sure to label each jar so you can compare the quantity and color of the water.

Summary of Results

Record your results on a chart like the one illustrated.

Recording chart for Experiment 2.

When you have finished, compare the amounts and colors of water in each jar. The darker the water, the more soil has run off. What have you discovered? Did the trays with leaf litter and grass have less runoff than the control tray? Did the tray with grass have less runoff than the tray with leaf litter? Was your hypothesis correct? Fill in your chart carefully and summarize what you found.

Tray	Description	Water color	Water (run-off) volume in tablespoons or oz.
1	soil		
2	leaf litter		
3	grass		

Troubleshooter's Guide

Below are some problems that may arise during this experiment, some possible causes, and some ways to remedy the problems.

Problem: The grass did not grow.

Possible cause: Perhaps there was too much or too little light or water, or the temperature was too cold or too hot. Adjust these conditions and plant some more grass seed. If this fails, try another kind of seed.

Problem: Soil is sliding down the trays when they are inclined.

Possible cause: The incline of your trays is too steep. Try lowering the support on which you are resting your trays.

Problem: No water is running off.

Possible cause: You are not using enough water for the amounts and kind of soil you are using. Use more water, but be sure you use the same amount for all of your trials.

Problem: All the water is the same color.

Possible cause: The grass and leaf cover are not thick enough to show a difference from the control tray. Add more leaf litter to Tray 2 and try again. Add more grass seed to Tray 3 and continue watering all three trays until the grass grows more thickly. Then try the erosion test again.

Change the Variables

You can vary this experiment by changing the variables. There are several possibilities. For example, you could cover the trays of soil with different amounts of leaf litter and compare the effect on erosion. When there is more leaf litter, is there less erosion?

You could also try growing other types of plants. For instance, what is the difference in the amount of runoff from a tray with bean plants versus a tray with grass? You might want to combine several types of plants. Some plants have extensive root systems, while other plants have broad leaves. Which characteristic seems to make a greater difference in preventing erosion?

Another way to change the variables is to prop a tray at an angle and try **terracing** the soil (forming "steps" with the soil). If you plant grass on terraced soil, how does the amount of runoff compare with the amount from a tray of grass that was grown on one level?

Design Your Own Experiment

How to Select a Topic Relating to this Concept

If you are interested in erosion or its effects, you can create many fascinating experiments. For example, you could study the effects on erosion of different kinds of plants growing in the soil. How about the difference between the size or age of plants? Or the number of plants growing in one place?

Or perhaps you are interested in the effects of human development (building) on erosion. What are the effects of concrete or pavement? What are the effects of deforestation or drainage of wetlands?

Erosion can also be caused by wind or ice. What would happen if you blew a fan over different kinds of soils?

Check the For More Information section and talk with your science teacher or school or community media specialist to start gathering information on erosion questions that interest you. You may also want to find out if there is an Agricultural Research Station or Cooperative Extension Office near you. If so, they can tell you about local erosion problems and projects.

Steps in the Scientific Method

To do an original experiment, you need to plan carefully and think things through. Otherwise you might not be sure what question you are answering, what you are or should be measuring, or what your findings prove or disprove.

Here are the steps in designing an experiment:

- State the purpose of—and underlying question behind—the experiment you propose to do.

- Recognize the variables involved, and select one that will help you answer the question at hand.
- State a testable hypothesis, an educated guess about the answer to your question.
- Decide how to change the variable you selected.
- Decide how to measure your results.

Recording Data and Summarizing the Results

Your data should include charts, such as the one you did for these experiments. They should be clearly labeled and easy to read. You may also want to include photos, graphs, or drawings of your experimental setup and results.

If you are preparing an exhibit, you may want to bring in some of your actual results, such as jars of water or soil clearly labeled with their origins. If you have done a nonexperimental project, you will want to explain clearly what your research question was and provide illustrations of your findings.

Related Projects

You can design projects that are similar to these experiments, involving trials and charts of data to summarize your results. You could also prepare a model that demonstrates a point you are interested in with regard to erosion or its effects. Or you could do an investigation into agricultural or building considerations that include erosion. You could do a research project on the environmental and ecological effects of erosion and present your findings in a poster or booklet. The possibilities are numerous.

For More Information

Environmental Defense Fund Worldwide. http://www.edf.org ❖ Current news relating to many environmental issues, including erosion.

Giono, Jean. *The Man Who Planted Trees.* White River Junction, VT.: Chelsea Green Publishing Company, 1985. ❖ Story about a man who single-handedly transformed his environment by planting trees over time.

Temperate Forests. New York: Habitat Ecology Learning Program, Wildlife Conservation Society, 1995. ❖ Provides activities for learning more about trees and forests and humans' impact on them.

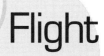

Flight

For birds, flight is moving through the air with wings; but for humans, flight is traveling through the air in an airplane. It is surprising that applying the dynamics of flight did not get off the ground earlier than the twentieth century, because the first human attempts to glide through the sky took place about 3,000 years ago in China using kites. It is recorded that in 196 B.C., General Han Hsin used kites to measure the distance to an enemy stronghold. Kites would later provide the key to wing performance principles used in the twentieth century airplane.

It's a bird, it's a man, it crashed . . .

In the eleventh century, an English inventor named Eilmer fastened wing mechanisms to his hands and feet and launched himself off a tower. Although Eilmer actually glided for a while before crashing, he broke both his legs and regretted forgetting to put a tail device on his back end. In the fifteenth century, Leonardo da

Words to Know

Aerodynamics:
The study of the motion of gases (particularly air) and the motion and control of objects in the air.

Centripetal force:
Rotating force that moves towards the center or axis.

Artist and scientist Leonardo da Vinci sketched a flying machine as early as the fifteenth century. (Photo Researchers Inc. Reproduced by permission.)

Otto Lilienthal made over 2,000 gliding experiments. (Corbis-Bettmann. Reproduced by permission.)

Vinci (1452–1519)—an Italian engineer, artist, inventor, theatrical designer, musician, and sculptor—drew one of the first sketches of a flying machine. His detailed drawing of a helicopter featured a wing and a horizontal propeller. Because da Vinci felt his painting should reflect light, space, and other sciences such as anatomy, he drew hundreds of sketches of nature and of inventions such as his flying machine.

The man who discovered lift

In the eighteenth century, Daniel Bernoulli (1700–1782)—a Swiss mathematician, botanist, and anatomist—discovered that force arises from differences in pressure as objects move through a gas or liquid. Bernoulli's discovery later was used to explain what gives birds their **lift,** or ability to glide without falling. His theory would later be used in the design of the airplane.

Making the "Wright" connection

By the end of the nineteenth century, several people had made significant headway in developing the airplane. But it was Wilbur and

(Words to Know)

Control experiment:
A set-up that is identical to the main experiment but not affected by the variable being tested in the main experiment. Results from the control experiment are compared to results from the actual experiment to determine the effect of the variable.

Orville Wright who put all the pieces together to create an airplane that could fly.

Three men inspired the Wright brothers, setting the stage for this important invention. One was Otto Lilienthal, a German who made 2,000 unpowered flights with his glider. Another was Samuel Pierpont Langley, a prominent scientist and head of the Smithsonian Institution. Langley launched two model airplanes in 1896 that remained airborne long enough to impress the United States Army, which gave him $50,000 for his experiments. The third was Octave Chanute, an American who also conducted gliding experiments. Both Chanute and Lilienthal felt an aircraft's wings should be curved on top and concave underneath. This shape reduced air pressure above the wing and increased it below, providing the aircraft's lift. All three men wrote books about their theories and experiences.

The Wright brothers' historic first flight took place in 1903. (Photo Researchers Inc. Reproduced by permission.)

Words to Know

Hypothesis:
An idea in the form of a statement that can be tested by observations and/or experiment.

Lift:
Upward force on the wings of an aircraft created by differences in air pressure on top of and underneath the wings.

The Wright brothers were successful because they were able to control their aircraft once it flew, an accomplishment that other inventors had been unable to achieve. The key was twisting the wing tips to maintain balance, just as birds alter their wing shape to change flight direction. Beginning in 1899, these persistent, resourceful men pored over any aviation information they could get their hands on and became flying experts. As businessmen, they ran a small, successful bicycle shop in Dayton, Ohio. During off-hours, they tested airfoil sections in a homemade wind tunnel, designed a lightweight internal combustion gas engine, and experimented with kites and gliders. They spent hundreds of hours testing their findings in their shop, on empty fields, and in deserted windy areas like the sand dunes at Kitty Hawk, North Carolina. It was there, on December 17, 1903, their airplane soared for 12 seconds, traveling 120 feet (36 meters) before landing. It became the first flying machine to stay aloft on its own power with a passenger.

Making objects fly was a challenge to the early inventors. Performing basic experiments in **aerodynamics** will help you understand some of the basic principles of flight.

(W)ords to Know

Propeller:
Radiating blades mounted on a rapidly rotating shaft, which moves aircraft forward.

Turbulence:
Air disturbance that affects an aircraft's flight.

Variable:
Something that can change the results of an experiment.

Experiment 1
Lift-Off: How can a glider be made to fly higher?

Purpose/Hypothesis
In this experiment you will create an aerodynamic glider capable of moving through the air and modify it so it can soar higher, gaining lift by manipulating the wings. According to Bernoulli's principle, force arises from differences in pressure. Pilots change the degree of lift by manipulating the flaps on the wings' edges. To understand the effects of air pressure, examine the diagrams illustrated. Before you begin, make an educated guess about the outcome of this experiment based on your knowledge of flight. This educated guess, or prediction, is your **hypothesis.** A hypothesis should explain these things:

- the topic of the experiment
- the variable you will change
- the variable you will measure
- what you expect to happen

experiment
CENTRAL

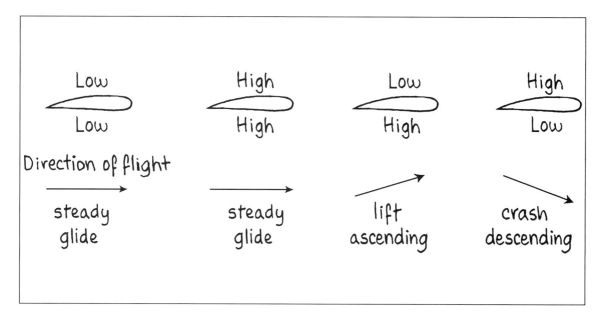

A hypothesis should be brief, specific, and measurable. It must be something you can test through observation. Your experiment will prove or disprove whether your hypothesis is correct. Here is one possible **hypothesis** for this experiment: "Modifying the wing cross-sectional shape will create more lift under the wing that will allow the glider to fly higher."

Air flows a greater distance over the top of a wing, creating low air pressure there. Higher air pressure under the wing forces the wing upward.

What Are the Variables?

Variables are anything that might affect the results of an experiment. Here are the main variables in this experiment:

- the type of balsa wood glider used (both gliders should be identical, simple, and lightweight)

- the type of modifications made to the wing shape of the second glider

In other words, the variables in this experiment are everything that might affect the flight time of the gliders. If you change more than one variable, you will not be able to tell which variable had the most effect on the gliders' flight.

In this case the **variable** you will change is the wing shape of one of the gliders, and the variable you will measure is the distance the gliders fly.

Level of Difficulty
Easy.

Materials Needed
- 2 balsa wood gliders (Styrofoam gliders are acceptable substitutes, but the gliders must have no propellers or landing gear.)
- 1 high power fan, 16 to 24 inches (41 to 61 cm) in diameter
- 2 pieces of string, 18 inches (45 cm) long
- 2 index cards, 4 x 6 inches (10 x 15 cm)
- 1 roll of adhesive tape

Approximate Budget
$5 for planes. (Borrow the fan from a family member or teacher.)

Timetable
30 minutes.

Step-by-Step Instructions
1. Prepare the control and test gliders. Assemble as shown on the packing bag.

2. Tie one string to the nose of each glider. If there is a metal or plastic clip on the nose, use it to attach the string.

3. Modify the wing of the test glider to create lift. Fold the top and bottom of the index card as shown in the diagram.

4. Tape the cards over the tops of the wings of the test glider.

5. Modify the index card. Push forward from the back of the wing so

 How to Experiment Safely

Use caution handling fans. Make sure the fan is unplugged when assembling the experimental apparatus and never touch the blades of the fan when it is operating.

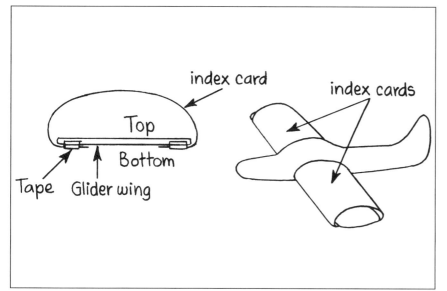

Steps 3 and 4: Closeup of index card folded over one glider wing and how the glider looks with the index cards on both wings.

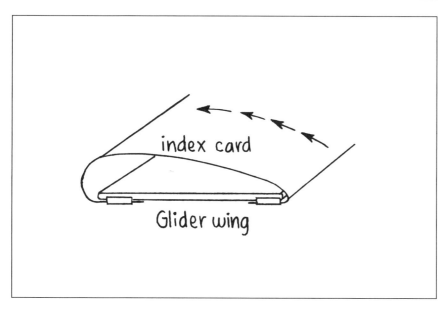

Step 5: Index card folded and modified to give lift.

that the bubble shape is toward the front of the wing. Once you bend the index card, it molds into the shape as illustrated.

6. Attach the two strings from the planes to the bottom of the fan or the fan grating. (Remember, use caution. Make sure fan is unplugged at this stage.) Aim the fan slightly down toward the surface the planes are resting on.

7. Turn the fan on low, then medium. Record your observations.

experiment
CENTRAL

Troubleshooter's Guide

Sometimes problems may arise during an experiment. Here's an example of a problem and what may be the cause.

Problem: The gliders will not stay in the air.

Possible cause: Gliders fly only for short periods because of invisible disturbances in the air, known as **turbulence.** For this reason, a glider cannot be expected to fly long distances.

Summary of Results

Record your results by describing how each glider moves in response to the air currents. The modified-wing glider, or test glider, should jump up and glide in the air. The other, the control glider, should constantly dive into the table and flip over. You can measure how high the gliders lift off the table with a ruler.

Change the Variables

To vary this experiment, use gliders made from different materials, such as Styrofoam or cardboard. Try different fan speeds and change the angle at which the wind hits the glider.

Experiment 2
Helicopters, Propellers, and Centripetal Force: Will it fly high?

Purpose/Hypothesis

Centripetal force is force exerted by a spinning object. When objects such as gyroscopes and tops are set in motion, their spinning creates centripetal force. This centripetal force is directed toward the center point of the spinning object. As centripetal force builds momentum, it creates balance. Helicopters rely on this balance and are designed to create centripetal force with their **propellers.** Before you begin, make an educated guess about the outcome of this experiment based on your knowledge of flight. This educated guess, or prediction, is your **hypothesis.** A hypothesis should explain these things:

What Are the Variables?

Variables are anything that might affect the results of an experiment. Here are the main variables in this experiment:

- the number and position of the dimes (weights) on the propellers

In other words, the variables in this experiment are everything that might affect the flight of the whirly toy. If you change more than one variable, you will not be able to tell which variable had the most effect on the toy's flight.

- the topic of the experiment
- the variable you will change
- the variable you will measure
- what you expect to happen

A hypothesis should be brief, specific, and measurable. It must be something you can test through observation. Your experiment will prove or disprove whether your hypothesis is correct. Here is one possible hypothesis for this experiment: "Centripetal force can be disturbed if the balance is disrupted, thus preventing flight."

In this case the **variable** you will change is the number and position of the dimes on the toy's propeller, and the variable you will measure is the toy's flight.

Level of Difficulty
Easy.

Materials Needed
- Whirly toy—a propeller on a stick
- 4 dimes
- 1 roll of adhesive tape
- meterstick

Approximate Budget
$3 for whirly toy.

How to Experiment Safely
Use caution when flying the toys. Avoid contact with eyes.

Timetable
20 minutes.

Step-By-Step Instructions

1. Spin the whirly toy between the palms of your hands and carefully release it.

2. Use the meterstick to record about how high the toy jumps.

3. Tape two dimes onto the propeller of the toy, repeat step 1, and measure the height of its flight. Record the height of the jumps.

4. Remove one of the dimes and test the toy's flight again. Use caution. The flight will be erratic. Record the change in balance and flight.

5. Repeat this test with the dimes in different positions, such as those illustrated.

LEFT: Example of a whirly toy, or propeller on a stick.

RIGHT: Step 3: Toy with dimes attached to each end of the propellers.

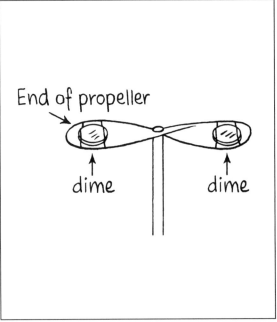

End of propeller

dime   dime

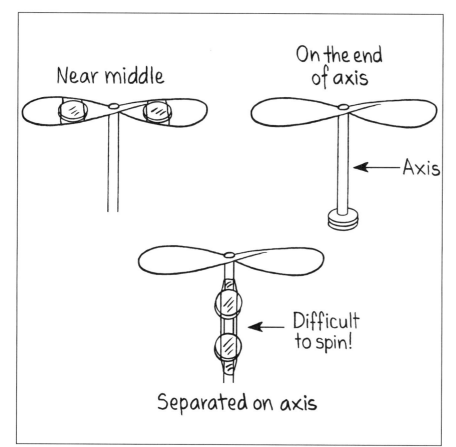

Near middle

On the end of axis

←——Axis

← Difficult to spin!

Separated on axis

Step 5: Toy with dimes taped in different positions. Test the flight patterns of each position.

Summary of Results

Reflect on your hypothesis. Did you discover centripetal force and the actions that can disrupt its effect or balance? Record your results in a

Troubleshooter's Guide

Here is a problem that may occur in your experiment and the possible cause for it.

Problem: The toy will not fly when the dimes are attached.

Possible cause: The dimes are too heavy. Try lightweight buttons that match each other in size and weight.

chart. Describe the behavior or draw what happened so others can learn from your experiment.

 **Design Your Own Experiment**

How to Select a Topic Relating to this Concept

Investigations and experiments in flight are exciting to explore. A toy box or toy store is a great place to discover objects capable of lift. Keep the ideas simple and work with objects familiar to you. Visit an aerospace museum, or try to arrange a personal tour at a local airport.

Check the For More Information section and talk with your science teacher or community media specialist to start gathering information on flight questions that interest you.

Steps in the Scientific Method

To do an original experiment, you need to plan carefully and think things through. Otherwise, you might not be sure what question you are answering, what you are or should be measuring, or what your findings prove or disprove.

Here are the steps in designing an experiment:

* State the purpose of —and the underlying question behind—the experiment you propose to do.
* Recognize the variables involved, and select one that will help you answer the question at hand.
* State a testable hypothesis, an educated guess about the answer to your question.
* Decide how to change the variable you selected.
* Decide how to measure your results.

Recording Data and Summarizing the Results

Ask your mom or dad to videotape the takeoff in the glider or pinwheel experiments. Or diagram the flight using photos. Keep the results and data charts simple and easy to use.

Related Projects

Air pressure is an invisible force that controls many objects and affects our lives. Simple experiments involving balloons or air bags can demonstrate the principles and power of air pressure.

For More Information

Leuzzi, Linda. *Transportation: Life in America 100 Years Ago.* New York: Chelsea House, 1995. ❖ Chronicles aircraft and people who were instrumental in furthering significant inventions.

Nahum, Andrew. *Flying Machine.* London: Dorling Kindersley, 1990. ❖ Covers aviation history, its inventors, and principles of flight.

Weiss, Harvey. *Strange and Wonderful Aircraft.* New York: Houghton Mifflin, 1995. ❖ Provides good background on aviation.

chapter 18

Germination

The first stage in the development of a seed, when it grows from seed to **seedling,** is **germination.** Like humans, seeds are equipped with their own growing mechanisms. An **embryo** and a supply of food exist within these tiny life starters. But until they are exposed to certain conditions of temperature, moisture, oxygen, and in some cases light, seeds remain **dormant,** or inactive, for days, months, or even hundreds of years. For example, scientists found a North American Arctic lupine seed that was about 10,000 years old. It was the oldest seed found so far, and it eventually grew into a plant similar to today's lupine. The seed waited 10,000 years and sprouted only when the right germination conditions were in place.

Really old books about green things

Botany, the study of plant life, had its beginnings in ancient Greece. Theophrastus (c. 372–287 B.C.) wrote two large botanical works that

A seed goes through several stages before it emerges as a seedling. (Photo Researchers Inc. Reproduced by permission.)

Words to Know

Botany:
The branch of biology involving the scientific study of plant life.

Chlorophyll:
A green pigment found in plants that absorbs sunlight, providing the energy used in photosynthesis, or the conversion of carbon dioxide and water to complex carbohydrates.

In the first stages of a seed's germination, the cotyledons start to use up stored food and its root system begins to grow. (Photo Researchers Inc. Reproduced by permission.)

(W)ords to Know

Cotyledon:
Seed leaves, which contain the stored source of food for the embryo.

Dormant:
The condition of a seed when its growing processes are inactive.

Embryo:
The seed of a plant, which through germination can develop into a new plant.

Germination:
The beginning of growth of a seed.

Hypothesis:
An idea in the form of a statement that can be tested by observation and/or experiment.

Micropyle:
Seed opening that enables water to enter easily.

Radicule:
Seed's root system.

were so revolutionary they guided scientists for the next 1,800 years. In his books *On the History of Plants* and *On Causes of Plants,* Theophrastus set down a theory of plant growth, plant structure analysis, and the relationship of agriculture to botany. He also identified, classified, and described 550 plants.

Getting through the ground

Germination begins with a seed's activation underground and ends when the first leaves push through the soil. A seed may remain **viable**, that is, capable of germination, for many years. Temperature plays a big factor in germination. The most favorable temperature ranges from 59°F to 100.4°F (15°C to 38°C). Temperatures above or below this range slow down the germination rate.

Absorbing water is a seed's first activity. Every seed has a little helper called a **micropyle**, an opening that enables water to enter the

experiment
CENTRAL

As they grow, seedlings use up much energy. As a result, they can actually push through tarred roads while growing. (Photo Researchers Inc. Reproduced by permission.)

seed more easily. Water kicks off the seed's life processes, including **res-piration.** Respiration is the process of oxygen from the air entering the seed and helping the cell use its stored food as energy. Too much water can literally drown out the necessary oxygen, so water has to be available in the right amount.

The embryo, including one or two **cotyledons,** or seed leaves, starts to use up its stored food. Its cells begin to divide and grow, which causes the seed's coat, or **testa,** to burst open. The seed's root system, or **radicule,** starts to grow, threading its way through the testa into the soil.

The cotyledon develops into the shape we call a seedling. It has two parts. The upper part supports an embryonic shoot at the end. This eventually pushes through the soil as a stem and leaves. The lower part contains the roots. As seeds grow, the stem and leaves push up. Food reserves provide the enormous energy they need to heave their way through soil. Seedlings have been known to push through tarred roads. Once they are above ground, **chlorophyll** usually begins to form in the leaves and stems.

Germination is the process a dormant seed goes through when it wakes up to begin the growing process. Our lives depend on plants. Conducting germination experiments will take the mystery out of this important life process.

Respiration:
The physical process that supplies oxygen to an animal's body. It also describes a series of chemical reactions that take place inside cells.

Seedling:
A small plant just starting to grow into its mature form.

Testa:
A tough outer layer that protects the embryo and endosperm of a seed from damage.

Variable:
Something that can affect the results of an experiment.

Viable:
The capability of developing or growing under favorable conditions.

experiment
CENTRAL

Experiment 1
Effects of Temperature on Germination: What temperatures encourage and discourage germination?

Purpose/Hypothesis

In this experiment you will investigate the ideal temperature needed to awaken a seed and stimulate it to grow. Before you begin, make an educated guess about the outcome of this experiment based on your knowledge of seed growth. This educated guess, or prediction, is your **hypothesis.** A hypothesis should explain these things:

- the topic of the experiment
- the variable you will change
- the variable you will measure
- what you expect to happen

A hypothesis should be brief, specific, and measurable. It must be something you can test through observation. Your experiment will prove or disprove whether your hypothesis is correct. Here is one possible **hypothesis** for this experiment: "Temperatures near or below freezing and those over 100°F will prevent germination."

In this case, the **variable** you will change is the temperature, and the variable you will measure is the number of seeds that germinate.

What Are the Variables?

Variables are anything that might affect the results of an experiment. Here are the main variables in this experiment:

- the temperature of the surrounding air
- the amount of water provided
- the type of soil used

In other words, the variables in this experiment are everything that might affect the germination of the seeds. If you change more than one variable, you will not be able to tell which variable had the most effect on the seeds' germination.

You expect those seeds stored in very hot and very cold temperatures will not germinate.

Level of Difficulty
Easy/moderate.

Materials Needed
- 15 seeds (Lima beans, kidney beans, and lentils are good seed choices; use only one variety.)
- water
- 3 sponges
- 3 plastic trays big enough to hold a sponge
- 3 napkins big enough to hold a sponge
- 3 thermometers (Fahrenheit or Celsius)
- access to a refrigerator
- a lamp with a 40-watt bulb

Approximate Budget
$10. (The seeds may be purchased at a supermarket as dried beans or you may find them in your family's kitchen. Try to borrow thermometers to reduce the cost.)

Timetable
20 minutes to set up the experiment; 1 to 2 weeks to complete it.

Step-by-Step Instructions
1. Place a sponge into each of the plastic trays.

2. Place five seeds on top of each sponge.

3. Pour water over the seeds and the sponge so that water collects in the tray. Do not pour too much. The seeds should not sit in the water.

4. Place a napkin over the seeds to keep them from drying out.

How to Experiment Safely
The lamp can cause fires when not handled properly. Ask an adult to help you set it up.

Steps 1 and 2: Set-up of plastic tray with sponge and five seeds on top of sponge.

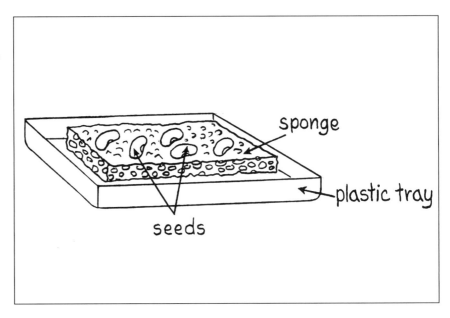

Steps 3 to 5: Set-up of plastic tray with napkin over seeds and thermometer.

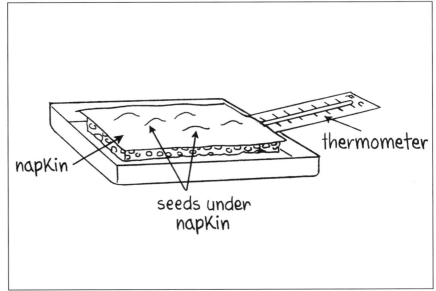

5. Place one tray indoors, away from a window or door. Place a thermometer under the napkin to record temperature.

6. Place another tray with seeds in the refrigerator. Again, place the thermometer under the napkin to record the temperature.

7. Place the third tray 10 to 12 inches (25 to 30 centimeters) away from the lamp and turn it on.

8. After about an hour, begin to record the temperature and condition of the seeds. Make up a data sheet with the headings Room Temperature and Location. Underneath add Date, Temperature, and Seed Activity. Then fill it in daily. Lift the napkin and diagram the changes in the seeds.

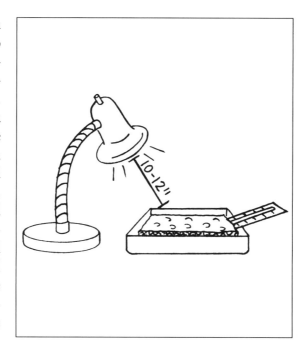

Step 7: Placement of third tray underneath the lamp.

9. Make sure the sponge stays wet at all times and the seeds are not under water. Check on the seeds daily.

Summary of Results

Compare the data on your chart and summarize your findings. Did the results support your hypothesis? Which tray of seedlings grew the most? Which tray of seedlings did not grow at all?

Troubleshooter's Guide

Here is a problem that may arise during this experiment, a possible cause, and a way to remedy the problem.

Problem: The sponge dries out too quickly.

Possible cause: There is not enough humidity. Cover the seeds with a loose layer of plastic wrap. This will increase humidity and prevent the seeds from drying out.

Change the Variables

To further explore how temperature affects germination, you can vary the experiment in the following ways:

- Use different types of seeds and see if one type of seed is more tolerant of high or low temperatures than others.
- Try growing seeds at different temperatures without watering them. Do any sprout?
- Try growing seeds in the dark at different temperatures. Cover the seed trays to block all light from reaching the seeds. Does light seem to be a factor in germination?

Experiment 2
Comparing Germination Times: How fast can seeds grow?

Purpose/Hypothesis

Each seed type has an average germination time. The seed waits for the correct conditions to occur. For example, if a seed emerged after the first warm day in spring, it might get caught by a late frost and die. So the seed may wait for consistent conditions that are ideal for growth.

What Are the Variables?

Variables are anything that might affect the results of an experiment. Here are the main variables in this experiment:

- the types of seeds used
- the temperature of the surrounding air
- the amount of water provided
- the type of soil used

In other words, the variables in this experiment are everything that might affect the time it takes for the seeds to germinate. If you change more than one variable, you will not be able to tell which variable had the most effect on the germination time.

experiment
CENTRAL

In this experiment, the goal is to compare the germination time for two different varieties of seeds. Before you begin, make an educated guess about the outcome of this experiment based on your knowledge of seed growth. This educated guess, or prediction, is your **hypothesis.** A hypothesis should explain these things:

- the topic of the experiment
- the variable you will change
- the variable you will measure
- what you expect to happen

A hypothesis should be brief, specific, and measurable. It must be something you can test through observation. Your experiment will prove or disprove whether your hypothesis is correct. Here is one possible hypothesis for this experiment: "When two different varieties of seeds are exposed to the same growing conditions, one group will consistently germinate before the other."

In this case, the **variable** you will change is the type of seed, and the variable you will measure is the time it takes to germinate. You expect one type of seed to germinate before the other.

Level of Difficulty

Easy/moderate. (Daily attention is required during the two-week experiment.)

Materials Needed

- 12 seeds—two different varieties; 6 lima bean seeds and 6 radish seeds
- 2 to 3 cups of potting soil
- egg carton (dozen size)
- water in a spray bottle
- tray big enough to hold the egg carton
- fork

Approximate Budget

$2 for seeds; borrow the spray bottle if possible.

Timetable

15 minutes to set up and 2 weeks to run the experiment.

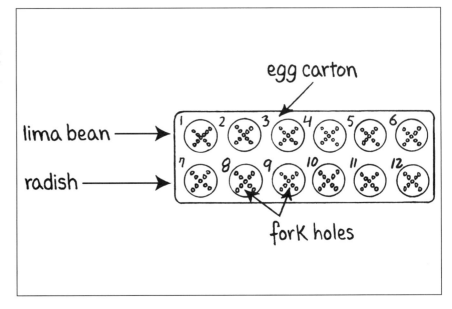

Steps 1 and 2: Set-up of drainage holes and seeds in the egg carton.

egg carton

lima bean →

radish →

fork holes

Step-by-Step Instructions

Step 7: Four views of egg carton wells as the seeds grow: no change, emergence of seedling, cotyledons open, and first true leaves open.

1. Use the fork to poke holes in the bottom of the wells in the egg carton. This will allow drainage. Label the wells with the numbers 1 to 12—1 to 6 along the back row and 7 to 12 along the front row.

2. Place the six lima bean seeds in the back row (wells 1 to 6) and the six radish seeds in the front row (wells 7 to 12).

N/C
(no change)

emergence
of seedlings

cotyledons
open

First true
leaves open

experiment
CENTRAL

Key:
- — N/C (no change)
- (symbol) Seedlings emerge
- (symbol) Cotyledons emerge
- (symbol) True leaves emerge

Seedlings

Seedling \ DAYS	1	2	3	4	5	6	7	8	9	10
1	N/C									
2	N/C	—	—							
3	N/C	—	—	—	(seedlings emerge)	(cotyledons emerge)	(true leaves emerge)			
4	N/C	—	—							
5	—	—	—							
6	—	—	—							
7	—	—	—							
8	—	—	—							
9	—	—	—							
10	—	—	—							
11	—	—	—							
12	—	—	—							

DAYS

3. Fill the wells with soil to the top. (Each seed should have the same amount of soil in the well.) Place the egg carton on the tray.

4. Using the spray bottle, water each well with the same number of squirts. Make sure all the soil is wet.

5. Place the egg carton/tray on a window sill in a warm room.

6. Water daily, making sure the soil stays wet.

7. Perform a daily inspection of your seedlings. Record the results on a chart with your observations. Number across the top from 1 to 12, with columns underneath. Then number the days down the far left of the chart, from 1 to 10. Use symbols illustrated to depict the stage of germination that is occurring.

Summary of Results

The goal of this experiment is to compare the average time of germination (from beginning to emergence of the first true leaves) for each seed species. Look at your results chart and determine the average number of days it took for the first true leaves to appear for each seed type. Which seeds germinated faster? Did one group consistently germinate before the other?

Change the Variables

To further explore seed germination times, change the environmental conditions under which you try to sprout the seeds. In separate experiments, vary the amount of water, sunlight, or warmth provided for one type of seed, such as radish seeds. Do radish seeds sprout more

Troubleshooter's Guide

Here is a problem that may arise in your experiment, a possible cause, and ways to remedy it.

Problem: The seeds have not done anything for two weeks.

Possible cause: They may need more water. Try increasing the water and storing them in a warmer location. If that does not work, replace the seeds with new ones.

quickly under certain environmental conditions? Then repeat the experiments with seeds of another type, such as bean seeds. Or you might expose identical trays of radish seeds and bean seeds to the same harsh environmental conditions (little water, cold temperatures) to see which seeds sprout first.

 # Design Your Own Experiment

How to Select a Topic Relating to this Concept

Since germination is dependent on so many variables, looking at variables may be the best place to start. For instance, cotyledons are the stored source of food for the growing embryo. What would happen if one cotyledon was removed? Or what would happen if a seed was cooked in boiling water for a minute? What would happen if the seed coat was removed before germination? Choose an aspect that interests you, then proceed with the research.

Check the For More Information section and talk with your science teacher or school or community media specialist to start gathering information on germination questions that interest you.

Steps in the Scientific Method

To do an original experiment, you need to plan carefully and think things through. Otherwise, you might not be sure what question you are answering, what you are or should be measuring, or what your findings prove or disprove.

Here are the steps in designing an experiment:

*   State the purpose of—and the underlying question behind—the experiment you propose to do.
*   Recognize the variables involved, and select one that will help you answer the question at hand.
*   State a testable hypothesis, an educated guess about the answer to your question.
*   Decide how to change the variable you selected.
*   Decide how to measure your results.

Recording Data and Summarizing the Results

As a scientist investigating a question, you must gather information and share it with others. Bring all the data together and write a conclusion. Simplify the data into charts or graphs for others to understand easily.

Related Projects

When dealing with seeds, you can take many different routes. You can try growing experiments or your investigation can be about seed anatomy, seed type (monocot or dicot), or methods of spreading the seeds.

For More Information

Burnie, David. *Plant.* London: Dorling Kindersley, 1989. ❖ Includes chapters on plant life processes such as "A Plant Is Born," which covers germination.

The Visual Dictionary of Plants. London: Dorling Kindersley, 1992. ❖ Offers an in-depth overview of plants and their activities through text and clear, detailed photos.

experiment
CENTRAL

chapter 19

Gravity

Earth orbits the Sun. The Moon orbits the Earth. But how do the planets stay in the sky? How do we stay on Earth's surface? Englishman Sir Isaac Newton (1642–1727) figured out the answers to these questions while watching an apple fall in his orchard. Newton reasoned that the force that pulls the Moon into its curved path around Earth instead of a straight line was the same force that pulled the apple to the ground. Newton was a scientist and mathematician, and he wrote his theory on a scrap of paper, something he did with all his thoughts and formulas. The falling apple initiated his famous **universal law of gravity**, which states that the attracting force between any two bodies is directly proportional to the product of their masses and inversely proportional to the square of the distance between them. It was published in his book *Principia* in 1687.

Well, how *do* they stay up there?

Danish scientist Tycho Brahe (1571–1630)

Sir Isaac Newton developed the theory of gravity as he watched an apple fall. (Library of Congress.)

Words to Know

Acceleration:
The rate at which the velocity and/or direction of an object is changing with the respect to time.

Elliptically:
An orbital path which is egg-shaped or resembles an elongated circle.

Hypothesis:
An idea in the form of a statement that can be tested by observation and/or experiment.

The planets in the Andromeda Galaxy, M31, follow an elliptical orbit. (Photo Researchers Inc. Reproduced by permission.)

developed a theory of planetary motions. Then, in 1609, Johannes Keppler used Brahe's theory when he said that the planets orbited **elliptically** rather than in a circle. An elliptical orbit is a curved path similar to the shape of an egg. Newton's laws unlocked many answers to questions scientists had been struggling with as they tried to figure out, among other things, what kept the planets orbiting in the first place.

The planets orbit and position themselves according to a balanced set of natural laws. One law is called **inertia,** the tendency of objects to continue whatever motion is affecting them. In other words, a rotating planet continues to rotate; a stationary book remains sitting on a desk. These objects continue to do what they do until a force causes an **acceleration** or change in their state of motion. This was part of Newton's First Law. In Newton's Second Law, he said the greater the force, the greater the acceleration. He also introduced the concept of **mass,** the amount of atoms, in an object. The relationship between an

OPPOSITE PAGE:
Newton discussed his theory about artificial earth satellites in his book System of the World *in the early eighteenth century. (Visual Archives. Reproduced by permission.)*

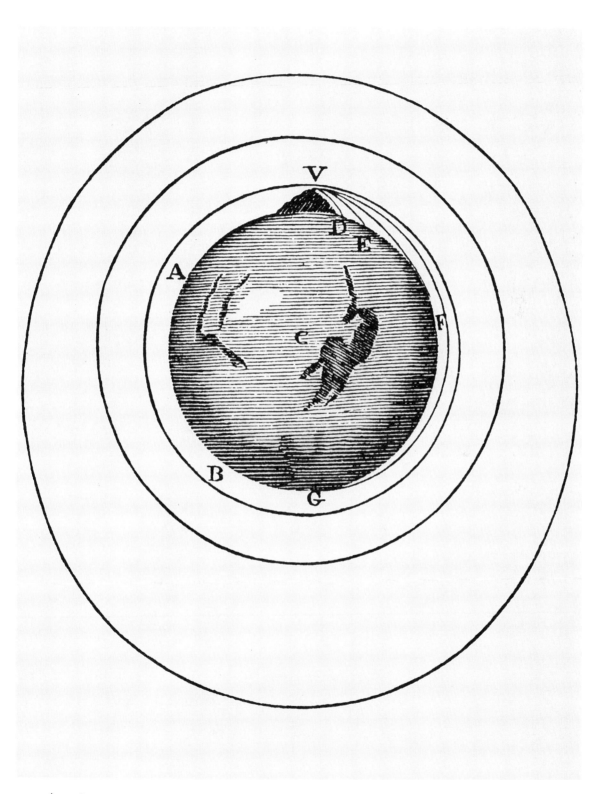

object's mass, acceleration, and the forces exerted on it was defined in his Second Law.

Newton's Third Law addressed gravity. For example, both the Moon and Earth are attracted to each other. But Earth has a much bigger mass, so it has a more powerful gravitational attraction that pulls the Moon into a curved path, or orbit, around Earth. The Sun exerts pulling forces as well. This attracting, pulling relationship exists between all the planets, moons, and stars. It keeps everything in the universe moving in an orderly fashion.

High tide
The gravitational forces of the Moon and Sun pull on Earth's surface water, causing tides, or water surges, twice a day. The Moon has a stronger gravitational pull because it is closer to Earth than the Sun. Twice a month, when the Sun, Moon, and Earth are aligned, the force of their gravitational pull causes the highest tides, called spring tides. When the Sun and Moon are at right angles, they pull in different directions and have a weaker gravitational pull. Then lower tides, called neap tides, take place.

What about me and the apple?
What keeps your feet on the ground is Earth's gravitational force pulling you down. The amount of gravitational force Earth exerts on an object, in this case you, depends on your mass. Earth has a very large mass, so its gravitational force is very strong. That is why we are not falling into space. You exert an attracting gravitational force on Earth as well, but the pull is very weak.

If *you* are being pulled to the ground, it is easy to understand why Earth's gravitational force also pulled Newton's apple to the ground. Gravitational forces have a great effect on our lives. Conducting experiments makes us aware of their presence and influence, from keeping us from falling off the planet to allowing us to launch rockets.

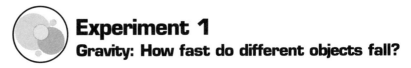

Experiment 1
Gravity: How fast do different objects fall?

Purpose/Hypothesis
In this experiment, you will determine the effect that mass has on the gravitational pull exerted on a falling object. You will drop three pen-

experiment
CENTRAL

cils taped together at the same time as you drop a single pencil to see whether the heavier group falls faster. You will also drop two objects of about the same weight (a pencil and a Ping-Pong ball) but with different shapes to see which falls faster.

According to the laws of physics, the falling rate for all objects is the same. Gravity does pull harder on objects with more mass. However, objects with more mass also have more inertia. Inertia causes objects to continue whatever motion is affecting them. That means objects at rest tend to stay at rest—they resist moving. The more mass an object has, the more inertia it has. The amount of force needed to overcome inertia balances out the pull of gravity, so objects with more mass fall at the same rate as objects with less mass.

Falling rates can also be affected by air resistance, the force that air exerts on a moving object. Air resistance pushes up on a falling object, while gravity pulls down. The more surface an object has, the more air resistance it has and the more slowly it will fall. You can test this by crumpling a sheet of paper into a ball and dropping it at the same time as you drop a flat sheet of the same paper. The flat sheet has more air resistance and will fall more slowly.

What Are the Variables?

Variables are anything that might affect the results of an experiment. Here are the main variables in this experiment:

- the weight of each pencil
- whether the pencils are dropped in a vertical or a horizontal position
- the distance from which all objects are dropped
- the amount of force used when the objects are dropped

In other words, the variables in this experiment are everything that might affect the mass and shape of the objects. If you change more than one variable, you will not be able to tell which variable had the most effect on the speed with which the objects hit the floor.

Before you begin the experiment, make an educated guess about the outcome based on your knowledge of gravity. This educated guess, or prediction, is your **hypothesis.** A hypothesis should explain these things:

- the topic of the experiment
- the variable you will change
- the variable you will measure
- what you expect to happen

A hypothesis should be brief, specific, and measurable. It must be something you can test through observation. Your experiment will prove or disprove your hypothesis. Here is one possible hypothesis for the pencil experiment: "The group of pencils and the single pencil will fall at the same rate." For the Ping-Pong ball experiment, your hypothesis might be this: "The Ping-Pong ball will fall more slowly than the pencil because its shape gives it more air resistance."

In this case, the variable you will change is the mass (pencils) and the shape (pencil and Ping-Pong ball) of the objects. The variable you will measure or observe is the time when each object hits the floor.

Level of Difficulty
Easy/moderate.

Materials Needed
- 4 wooden pencils, unsharpened
- masking tape
- 1 Ping-Pong ball
- 6-foot (1.8 m) step ladder

Approximate Budget
$5 for pencils, tape, and Ping-Pong ball.

Timetable
20 minutes.

How to Experiment Safely

Ask an adult to climb the ladder so you can lie on the floor and observe when the objects hit the floor. No one should ever stand on the top step of a ladder.

Step-by-Step Instructions

1. Tape three of the pencils together tightly.

2. Place the taped pencils and the single pencil on the top of the ladder.

3. Ask your adult helper to climb the ladder.

4. Position yourself flat on the floor,

Grouping of Pencils

LEFT: Step 1: Tape three of the pencils together tightly.

BELOW: Steps 3 to 6: Adult drops pencils from ladder; student positioned on floor to observe.

Dropping the Pencils

about 6 feet (1.8 m) from the ladder so you can observe the pencils hitting the floor.

5. Have the adult pick up the taped pencils in one hand and the single pencil in his or her other hand.

6. Have the adult hold both sets of pencils at the same height from the floor, in a vertical position, and drop them. Your helper should not use any force, but simply let them both go at the same time.

7. Ask the adult to help you repeat this procedure with different groupings of pencils. Record your observations in a table similar to the one illustrated.

8. Have the adult repeat the procedure, dropping a single pencil, held vertically to reduce air resistance, and the Ping-Pong ball. Observe which object hits the floor first.

Summary of Results

Step 7: Results chart for Experiment 1.

Study the observations on your table and decide whether your hypotheses were correct. Did the taped pencils and the single pencil hit

Results Chart

Pencil Grouping	Falling Rate
3 grouped pencils and 1 pencil	same
2 grouped pencils and 2 loose pencils	
4 loose pencils	

experiment
CENTRAL

the floor at the same time? If not, how would you explain the difference? (The larger group of pencils would have slightly more air resistance than the single pencil, even when dropped in vertical positions.)

Did the single pencil hit the floor before the Ping-Pong ball? Why is that? Write a paragraph summarizing your findings and explaining whether they support your hypothesis.

Change the Variables
Here are some ways you can vary this experiment:

*   Vary the distance from which you drop the objects. Can you observe a difference in falling rates when the distance is longer or shorter?
*   Try dropping other objects with different amounts of mass or the same mass but different shapes. See how these changes affect their falling rates.

Project 2
Measuring Mass: How can a balance be made?

Purpose
A useful measurement for science is not the **weight** but the mass of an object. The mass is the amount of atoms that make up an object. Here is your hypothesis: "By creating a balance with counterweights, you will cancel out the effects of gravity and calculate the mass of an object."

The materials used as a counterweight can be varied if the mass is known. The balance you will create is accurate only for low-mass objects. Do not exceed .9 of an ounce (25 grams) or accuracy will diminish.

Level of Difficulty
Moderate.

Materials Needed
*   two 5-ounce (148-ml) cups
*   plastic ruler, 1 foot (30 cm) long
*   dried beans
*   quarter, penny, nickel
*   30 small metal paper clips
*   pencil
*   Optional: dried split peas, Popsicle sticks

Approximate budget

$4 for the beans and wood.

Timetable

Approximately 30 minutes.

Step-by-Step Instructions

1. Place the pencil on a level desk. If the pencil rolls, the desk is not level.

2. Mark the ruler in the middle.

Recording chart for Project 2.

3. Place the ruler over the pencil at right angles, as illustrated.

Object	Counterweights	Total mass

experiment
CENTRAL

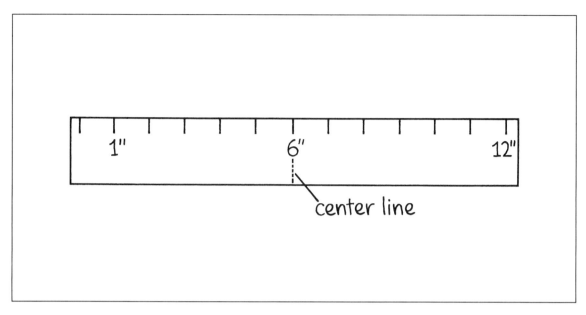

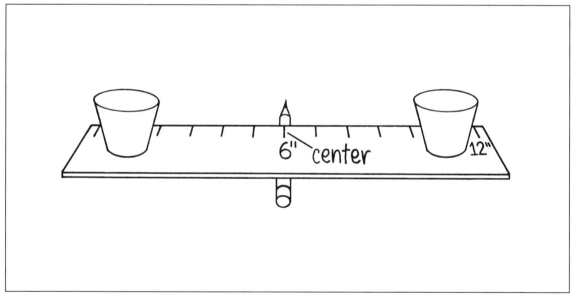

4. At each end of the balance place the 5-ounce (148 milliliter) paper cups. Draw rings to mark their positions.

5. Make sure the ruler is level, and neither side is touching the table-top.

6. If a side is touching, very *slightly* move the ruler as it rests on the pencil. Try to balance it perfectly.

TOP: Step 2: Mark the ruler in the middle.

BOTTOM: Steps 3 and 4: Place the ruler over the pencil at right angles. At each end of the balance place the 5-ounce paper cups.

experiment
CENTRAL

Below is a list of common materials and their mass:

    nickel— .175 oz. (5 grams)
    dime —.08 oz. (2.3 grams)
    penny —.087 oz. (2.5 grams)
    quarter —.19 oz. (5.5 grams)
    wooden Popsicle stick —.05 oz. (1.5 grams)
    one paper clip —.018 oz. (0.5 grams)
    dried split pea —.003 oz. (0.1 gram)

7. As a test material, place a quarter (.19 oz or 5.5 grams) in one cup.

8. Place 1 nickel (.175 oz. or 5 grams) and one paper clip (.018 oz. or 0.5 grams) in the other cup. The balance should be level.

9. Continue to test other combinations of materials to determine which have equal mass.

Summary of Results

You now have made an instrument of measurement. It is important that you keep a record of the standard measurements and items for counterweights. Illustrated on page 286 is a chart that you can make to keep track of the mass of tested objects.

 Troubleshooter's Guide

Below are some problems that may occur during this project, possible causes, and ways to remedy the problems.

Problem: When you tested the quarter, it did not balance.

Possible cause: The balance is not accurate to the .5 gram point. The actual mass of the quarter is 5.6 grams. Try adding one or two split peas to counter the weight.

Problem: The balance keeps tipping and it does not seem to level out.

Possible cause: Try using a pencil that has flattened sides to decrease sensitivity.

Design Your Own Experiment

How to Select a Topic Relating to this Concept

Gravity is a force of nature that can be examined and studied in many different ways. Pretend to be Newton and make observations about what happens around you. Notice common events. Why does a coin fall through water more slowly than through air? Is gravity the same in water as it is in air? The study of gravity will lead you into other areas of physics such as friction, buoyant force, and acceleration.

Steps in the Scientific Method

To do an original experiment, you need to plan carefully and think things through. Otherwise, you might not be sure what question you are answering, what you are or should be measuring, or what your findings prove or disprove.

Here are the steps in designing an experiment:

- State the purpose of—and the underlying question behind—the experiment you propose to do.
- Recognize the variables involved, and select one that will help you answer the question at hand.
- State a testable hypothesis, an educated guess about the answer to your question.
- Decide how to change the variable you selected.
- Decide how to measure your results.

Recording and Summarizing Results

It is important to be able to share your results with others. Put any data you collect into charts or graphs. Even Newton wrote down his measurements in journals.

When summarizing the results, reflect on your question or purpose and describe how it was answered or proven. Look at your hypothesis and see if your initial idea was correct. Plot the results on graphs and charts. Make them easy for others to understand or follow.

Related Projects

One type of experiment that would be fun might be a scale to measure weight. All you need is a spring, hook, and some cardboard. By hanging objects on the hook and hanging them on the spring, you can measure the pull of gravity on a mass.

For More Information

Allaby, Michael, et al. *The Visual Encyclopedia of Science.* New York: Kingfisher, 1994. ❖ Includes illustrated science text and colorful photos that explain the gravity concept.

Asimov, Isaac. *Asimov's Chronology of Science and Discovery.* New York: Harper & Row, 1989. ❖ Offers a clear, direct explanation of gravity.

Magill, Frank N. *The Great Scientists.* Danbury, CT: Grolier Education Corp., 1989. ❖ Contains a good background chapter about Isaac Newton, his discovery of gravity, and other scientific theories he introduced.

chapter 20

Greenhouse Effect

In 1827, a French mathematician named Jean-Baptiste-Joseph Fourier came up with an interesting theory. He said Earth's **atmosphere** protected its inhabitants against the freezing temperatures of space. Fourier pointed out that Earth's atmosphere acted as an **insulator,** an effect similar to what happens when heat is trapped within the glass walls and roof of a greenhouse. He called his theory the **greenhouse effect.**

Today we know that the greenhouse effect takes place when sunlight passes through the atmosphere and is absorbed by land and water. The energy in the sunlight is converted to heat energy to warm the surface of Earth. Some of this heat energy is re-radiated out into the atmosphere in the form of **infrared radiation.** The infrared radiation has a longer wavelength than the sunlight and is absorbed by certain gases in the atmosphere, such as carbon dioxide. This traps the heat, keeping Earth's surface warm. The greenhouse effect is actually a good thing. Without it, we would experience an average temperature of −2.2°F (−19°C), and we would all freeze.

Perfecting a theory

Two scientists in the nineteenth century expanded Fourier's theory. In 1861, English physicist John Tyndall said that certain atmospheric gases, such as carbon monoxide and water vapor, warmed Earth's surface. In 1896, Swedish scientist Svante Arrhenius made the greenhouse theory clearer in a scientific article. He stated that increased carbon dioxide levels in the atmosphere could trap more of the heat energy rising from Earth. More trapped heat energy meant warmer temperatures

Words to Know

Atmosphere:
Layers of air that surround Earth.

By-products:
Something produced in the making of something else.

Combustion:
Any chemical reaction in which heat, and usually light, are produced. The most common form of combustion is when organic substances combine with oxygen in the air to burn and form carbon dioxide and water vapor.

A greenhouse traps the Sun's heat within its glass walls and roof, just as carbon dioxide does in Earth's atmosphere. (Peter Arnold Inc. Reproduced by permission.)

on Earth's surface. Arrhenius was the first to understand the concept of **global warming** and climate changes because of the greenhouse effect.

We are all affected by the greenhouse effect

The greenhouse effect has been in the news a lot lately. Why? Carbon dioxide levels began to rise during the late 1700s when machines began doing work that had previously been done by humans and animals. The machines needed fuel to work, and **fossil fuels**, such as coal and wood, were used. Fossil fuels contain carbon. Burning these fuels releases the carbon, which combines with the oxygen in air to form carbon dioxide. Back in the 1700s, this was not a big problem because there were not as many people or machines. But today, burning fossil fuels such as gasoline has caused a critical situation.

Besides being used in vehicles—including cars, trucks, and planes—fossil fuels are used to produce electricity. Burning these fossil

fuels releases billions of tons (metric tons) of carbon dioxide into the air every year. At the same time, many of the forests, which absorb carbon dioxide from the air, have been cut down. All of these factors increase the volume of heat-trapping carbon dioxide gas in our atmosphere.

Global warming, caused by the greenhouse effect, causes polar ice caps and glaciers to melt faster. (Photo Researchers Inc. Reproduced by permission.)

In addition, water vapor in the air and about thirty other gases also trap Earth's heat, including gases from nitrogen-based fertilizers and methane emissions from decomposing vegetation.

experiment
CENTRAL

Nitrogen-based fertilizers contribute to the greenhouse effect. (Photo Researchers Inc. Reproduced by permission.)

These **greenhouse gases** absorb heat energy from Earth before it escapes into space. According to scientists, these heat-trapping gases will cause an average temperature rise of 3 to 8°F (16 to 13°C) in the next 60 years, which could cause destructive weather changes.

Conducting experiments and projects on how the greenhouse effect works will help you become aware of the delicate natural balance that maintains Earth's environment as we know it. We have already experienced some of the problems caused by an overload of greenhouse gases, including air pollution, which causes respiratory problems. Being more aware of the greenhouse effect may make you want to help reduce these gases and help our planet.

Words to Know

Global warming:
Warming of Earth's atmosphere as a result of an increase in the concentration of gases that store heat, such as carbon dioxide.

Greenhouse effect:
The warming of Earth's atmosphere due to water vapor, carbon dioxide, and other gases in the atmosphere that trap heat radiated from Earth's surface.

Greenhouse gases:
Gases that absorb infrared radiation and warm the air before the heat energy escapes into space.

Experiment 1
Creating a Greenhouse: How much will the temperature rise inside a greenhouse?

Purpose/Hypothesis

In this experiment you will measure the temperature inside a greenhouse. A greenhouse is a small enclosure that maintains a **microclimate** that is warmer than the climate outside it. A greenhouse is often used for growing plants in cold weather. It is made of plastic or glass that allows the Sun's light energy to pass through. When the light energy is absorbed by the soil and plants inside, it warms them. Some of this energy is then re-radiated out into the greenhouse in the form of infrared radiation, or heat energy. Because the heat energy has a longer wavelength than the entering light energy, most of the energy is absorbed and trapped by the plastic or glass of the greenhouse walls and roof, just as the greenhouse gases in our atmosphere absorb and trap the heat energy from Earth. Although a small portion of the heat energy escapes, most of it is reflected or re-radiated back into the greenhouse to warm the air.

Before you begin, make an educated guess about the outcome of this experiment based on your knowledge of greenhouses and the greenhouse effect. This educated guess, or prediction, is your **hypothesis.** A hypothesis should explain these things:

* the topic of the experiment
* the **variable** you will change
* the variable you will measure
* what you expect to happen

How a greenhouse works.

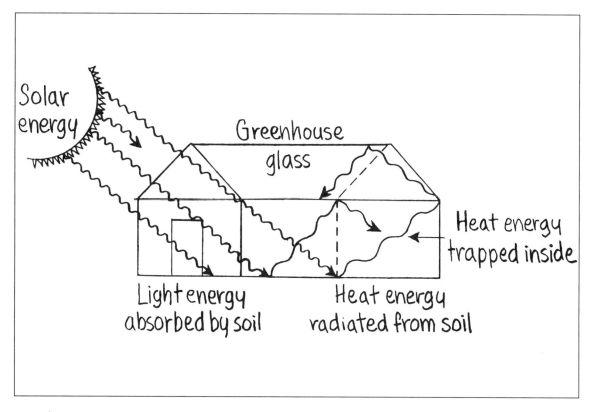

 What Are the Variables?

Variables are anything that might affect the results of an experiment. Here are the main variables in this experiment:

- the amount of sunlight reaching the greenhouse
- the amount of sunlight that passes through the glass or plastic
- the amount of wind or rain
- the color of the material under the greenhouse

In other words, the variables in this experiment are everything that might affect the temperature inside the greenhouse. If you change more than one variable, you will not be able to tell which variable had the most effect on temperature.

Words to Know

Hypothesis:
An idea in the form of a statement that can be tested by observation and/or experiment.

Infrared radiation:
Electromagnetic radiation of a wavelength shorter than radio waves but longer than visible light that takes the form of heat.

Insulation:
A material that is a poor conductor of heat or electricity.

Microclimate:
A unique climate that exists only in a small, localized area.

Troposphere:
Atmospheric layer closest to Earth where all life exists.

Variable:
Something that can change the results of an experiment.

A hypothesis should be brief, specific, and measurable. It must be something you can test through observation. Your experiment will prove or disprove whether your hypothesis is correct. Here is one possible hypothesis for this experiment: "The more sunlight that shines on the greenhouse, the higher the inside temperature compared to the outside temperature."

In this case, the variable you will change (or let nature change) is the amount of sunlight that reaches the greenhouse, and the variable you will measure is the temperature inside the greenhouse compared to the outside temperature. If the difference between the inside temperature and outside temperature is greater on days when more sunlight reaches the greenhouse, you will know your hypothesis is correct.

Level of Difficulty

Easy/moderate.

Materials Needed

- 2 thermometers
- 4 wooden boards, roughly 1 x 6 x 20 inches (2.5 x 15 x 50 centimeters)
- One 24 x 24-inch (60 x 60-centimeter) piece of transparent plastic or glass, 0.25 inch (0.5 centimeter) thick

 How to Experiment Safely
Goggles and adult supervision are required when hammering the nails. Wear gloves when handling the glass.

- Eight 2-inch (5-centimeter) nails
- hammer
- goggles
- gloves

Approximate Budget
$10. (Use any lumber that is cost-effective.)

Timetable
One week. (This experiment requires a half-hour to assemble and one week to monitor.)

Step-by-Step Instructions
1. Hammer two nails through each end of a piece of wood, as illustrated. Repeat with a second piece of wood. Place the wood into a square with the two pieces with nails opposite each other.

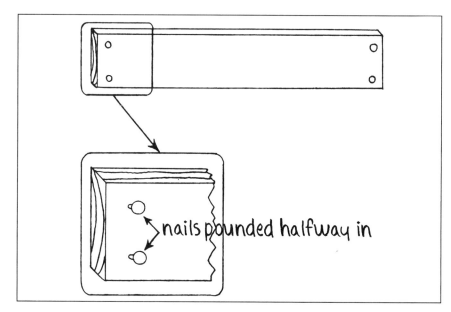

nails pounded halfway in

Step 1: Carefully hammer two nails through each end of a piece of wood.

2. Hold the wood in position and assemble the box by carefully driving the nails into the ends of the two remaining pieces of wood.

3. Place the piece of plastic or glass over the wood box. Be sure it completely overlaps the wood box so there are no gaps around the edges.

Step 6: Sample recording chart for Experiment 1.

4. Place the greenhouse outside in a sunny spot. Put one thermometer inside the greenhouse and one outside the greenhouse close by.

Greenhouse			
WEATHER CONDITIONS	DAY 1	DAY 2	DAY 3...
MORNING TEMP.	65	65	63
AFTERNOON TEMP.	75	76	76
EVENING TEMP.	65	65	66

Outside			
WEATHER CONDITIONS	DAY 1	DAY 2	DAY 3...
MORNING TEMP.	59	62	55
AFTERNOON TEMP.	65 ☁	67 🌤	69 ☀
EVENING TEMP.	58 🌧	59 ☁	59

KEY TO WEATHER CONDITIONS

☀ Sunny   ☁🌧 Rainy

🌤 Partly Sunny   ☁ Windy

☁ Cloudy

5. Record the temperature inside and outside at the same time in the morning, afternoon, and evening for seven days. Record for a longer period if three or more days are mostly cloudy, windy, or rainy.

6. Record the general weather conditions during each day. See the results chart illustrated.

Summary of Results

Review the data collected at the same time of day. Graph this data so you can compare temperatures inside and outside of the greenhouse. Note the general weather conditions for each day on the graph. Do your results confirm your hypothesis? Was the temperature inside the greenhouse higher on days when there was more sunshine? Was it consistently higher than the temperature outside? Was the difference between the inside temperature and the outside temperature greatest when there was more sunshine?

Troubleshooter's Guide

Here are some problems that may arise during this experiment, possible causes, and ways to remedy the problems.

Problem: The temperature inside the greenhouse is going up too high, for example, 110°F (43°C).

Possible cause: If you conduct this experiment during the warm summer months, the temperature inside the greenhouse will soar. Try placing a large piece of thin white paper on top of the greenhouse to block some of the Sun's rays.

Problem: The evening temperature inside the greenhouse is always much higher than the outside temperature.

Possible cause: If you place the greenhouse on a dark surface, such as a brick patio or walkway, the dark materials will absorb heat during the day. That heat will remain trapped under the greenhouse to keep the inside warm in the evening, even when the outside temperature drops.

Change the Variables

You can change the variables and repeat this experiment. For example, you can vary the amount of sunlight reaching the greenhouse by placing one or more layers of thin tracing paper or wax paper over the glass. You can also vary the color of the material under the greenhouse by first placing the greenhouse on a white poster board and then on a black poster board. Does the black poster board absorb more incoming sunlight and make the temperature inside the greenhouse higher? If you place two bricks inside the greenhouse, will they absorb and retain enough heat to keep the greenhouse warm all night? To find out, you would have to take temperature measurements at various times between sundown and sunrise.

When you conduct further experiments, remember to change only one variable at a time or you will not be able to tell which variable affected the results.

Project 2
Fossil Fuels: What happens when fossil fuels burn?

Purpose

Fossil fuels, such as oil, coal, and natural gas, are used to warm the world we live in and move the machines that make life easier. However, for every advantage there usually is a disadvantage. That is what this project will demonstrate.

Many fossil fuels are hydrocarbons, which means they contain hydrogen and carbon. When these fossil fuels are burned during **combustion,** they combine with oxygen and other gases in the air to produce carbon dioxide, water vapor, and other **by-products** that may harm the environment or act as greenhouse gases. The combustion of fossil fuels is a major contributor to the greenhouse effect.

In this project you will observe how carbon dioxide and water vapor are produced during combustion. You will also look for evidence of free carbon before it combines with oxygen to form carbon dioxide.

Level of Difficulty

Moderate. (The experimenter must be mature and responsible when performing this project.)

Materials Needed

- 1 paraffin candle
- matches
- plate or candle holder
- metal spoon
- white index card
- goggles
- leather gloves

Approximate Budget

$1 for the candle; other items will likely be found in the home.

Timetable

10 minutes.

Step-By-Step Instructions

1. Place the candle in the holder or on the plate. Make sure it will not fall over.

2. Remove all nearby flammable materials.

3. Using the matches, light the candle and let it burn for a minute. (Ask for help if needed. An adult *must* be present.)

4. Wearing goggles and gloves, hold the rounded end of the spoon 1 inch (2.5 centimeters) above the flame. Notice if anything accumulates on the spoon. Hold it there 10 seconds or less. Caution! The spoon will get hot.

5. Next, place the spoon directly into the flame for 5 to 10 seconds and remove. Notice if anything accumulates. Caution! The spoon will be very hot.

How to Work Safely

This project *requires* adult permission and supervision. Always use caution when handling matches and candles. Wear goggles, remove loose clothing, and tie back long hair. Do not try this project with any other fuel source. Gasoline, kerosene, propane, lamp oil, and other fuels can be explosive and extremely dangerous.

petroleum fuel

water

$$C_2H_6 + O_2 \longrightarrow CO_2 + H_2O$$

oxygen

carbon dioxide gas

6. After the spoon has cooled, use your finger to transfer some of the black residue that has appeared on the spoon onto the index card. The residue is carbon produced by the combustion. Notice that the carbon was formed when the spoon was *inside* the flame. However, when you held the spoon *above* the flame, there was no black residue. A general formula for the combustion of paraffin-type hydrocarbons is illustrated above.

During the first stage of combustion, the carbon and hydrogen molecules in the paraffin split apart. So, inside the flame, the carbon is free and has not bonded to the oxygen yet. That is why the carbon collected on the spoon held in the flame. Once the carbon rises out of the flame, it joins with the oxygen in the air and becomes the invisible gas carbon dioxide.

7. Put on the goggles and gloves again and hold the glass upside down so the open end of the glass is even with the top of the candle, and the flame is inside the glass. Use both hands to hold the glass and keep it centered above the flame. Hold it there for 10 seconds or less. Caution! The glass will get hot. Watch for moisture accumulating inside the glass. This is the water vapor produced by the combustion.

Summary of Results

Make sure you keep a journal of your observations. Pay close attention to what is happening. If you do not give the project your full attention, you can miss events. You can diagram these events in a journal.

Design Your Own Experiment

How to Select a Topic Relating to this Concept

Since the atmosphere acts as a giant greenhouse, sheltering life on Earth from harsh environments in space, the atmosphere is a good starting point for experiments and projects. For example, you might begin with an investigation into the layers of the atmosphere and how

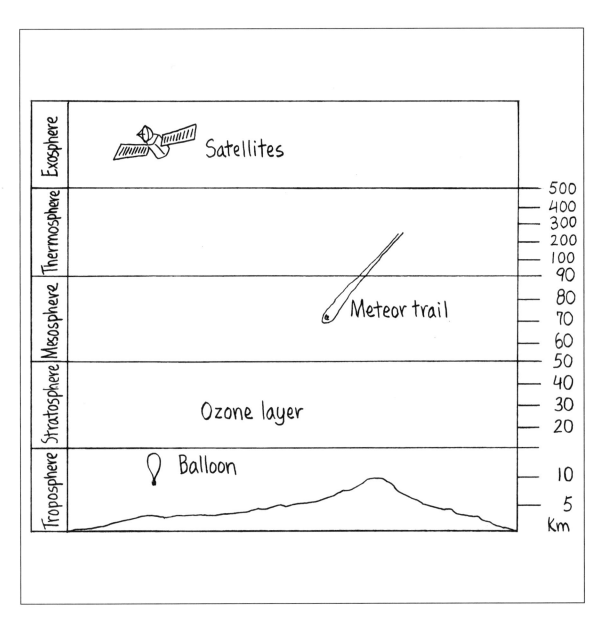

Layers of the atmosphere surrounding Earth.

they help insulate the earth. You might also identify which machines or sources of power generate the lowest levels of carbon dioxide and other greenhouse gases.

Check the For More Information section and talk with your science teacher or school or community media specialist to start gathering information on greenhouse effect questions that interest you. As you consider possible experiments and projects, be sure to discuss

experiment
CENTRAL

them with your science teacher or another knowledgeable adult before trying them. Some of them might be dangerous.

Steps in the Scientific Method

To do an original experiment, you need to plan carefully and think things through. Otherwise, you might not be sure what question you are answering, what you are or should be measuring, or what your findings prove or disprove.

Here are the steps in designing an experiment:

- State the purpose of—and the underlying question behind—the experiment you propose to do.
- Recognize the variable involved, and select one that will help you answer the question at hand.
- State a testable hypothesis, an educated guess about the answer to your question.
- Decide how to change the variable you selected.
- Decide how to measure your results.

Recording Data and Summarizing the Results

Your data on the greenhouse effect can be put into charts or graphs or even photographed to enable the information to be shared with others. After the data is collected and analyzed, your final responsibility is to make a conclusion based on your experiment and decide whether your hypothesis was true.

Related Projects

For atmospheric experiments, it's best to study the layer closest to earth called the **troposphere**. This layer is where all life exists. For instance, you could design an experiment with plants and insects living in an environment that has an altered atmosphere.

For More Information

Bilger, Burk. *Global Warming*. New York: Chelsea House Publishers, 1992. ❖ Examines the phenomenon of global warming, discussing the greenhouse effect in its positive, life-giving form and again as this mechanism is knocked out of balance.

Edelson, Edward. *Clean Air*. New York: Chelsea House Publishers, 1992. ❖ Discusses different types of pollutants and gases that can be found in the atmosphere and ways to clean up the air.

experiment
CENTRAL

Erickson, Jon. *Greenhouse Earth: Tomorrow's Disaster Today.* Blue Ridge Summit, PA: Tab Books, 1990. ❖ Provides an overview of how this phenomenon formed and the consequences.

Williams, Jack. *The Weather Book.* New York: Vintage Books, 1997. ❖ Includes diagrams and text on the greenhouse effect and other atmosphere-related phenomena.

chapter 21

Groundwater Aquifers

The term **groundwater** sounds as if it refers to an underground lake or river, but relatively little groundwater is found in this form. Groundwater lies below the surface of the land; in fact, it is almost everywhere underground. Mostly it is found in the tiny **pores,** or spaces, between rocks and particles of soil and in the cracks of larger rocks.

Where does groundwater come from? When rain falls, some of it flows along the surface of the ground into streams and lakes as **runoff.** Some of the rain evaporates into the atmosphere, some is taken up by plant roots, and some seeps into the ground to become groundwater.

Aquifers are like big sponges

Underground areas called **aquifers** collect much of this groundwater. An aquifer is composed of **permeable** rock, loose material that holds water. Permeable means "having pores that permit a liquid or a gas to pass through." You might think of a groundwater aquifer as a big sponge that soaks up the rain that seeps below the surface.

As water from the surface slowly seeps down, or **percolates,** through the soil, it eventually hits a solid, or **impermeable,** layer of rock or soil. The aquifer forms as groundwater collects in the area above this impermeable layer. The **water table** is the level of the upper surface of the groundwater. If the water table in an area is high, the upper surface of the groundwater is only a short distance below the surface of the ground.

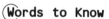

Words to Know

Aeration:
Mixing a gas, like oxygen, with a liquid, like water.

Aquifer:
Underground layer of sand, gravel, or spongy rock that collects water.

Artesian well:
A well in which water is forced out under pressure.

Coagulation:
A process during which solid particles in a liquid begin to stick together.

Confined aquifer:
An aquifer with a layer of impermeable rock above it where the water is held under pressure.

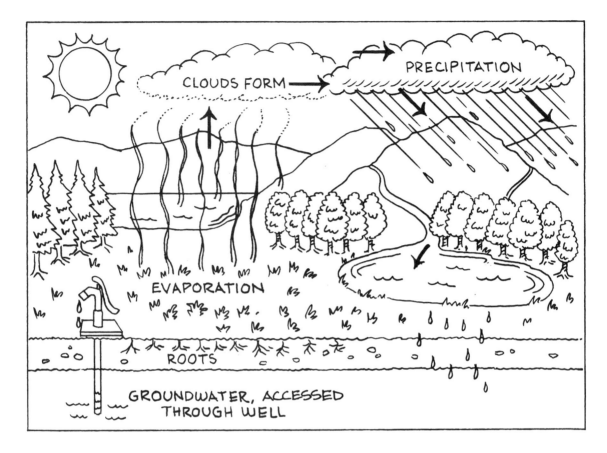

How groundwater forms.

Confined or unconfined?

Groundwater occurs in two conditions: confined and unconfined. A **confined aquifer** has a layer of impermeable clay or rock above it, and the water is held under pressure greater than the atmospheric pressure. When a well is drilled into a confined aquifer, it penetrates that impermeable, confining layer, allowing the water to rise under pressure. This is called an **artesian well**. An **unconfined aquifer** has no impermeable layer above it and is usually shallower than a confined aquifer.

How big is an aquifer?

The size of an aquifer depends on the amount of rainfall and the composition of the underground rock and soil. The world's largest aquifer is in the United States. Called the Ogallala, it spreads under eight western states, from South Dakota to Texas. The Ogallala formed millions of years ago and is still supplying water to cities, businesses, and farms. Unfortunately, people are using water from the Ogallala faster than it can be naturally replenished, and the water table is falling.

ⓦords to Know

Disinfection:
Using chemicals to kill harmful organisms.

Filtration:
Removing impurities from a liquid with a filter.

Groundwater:
Water that soaks into the ground and is stored in the small spaces between the rocks and soil.

Impermeable:
Not allowing substances to pass through.

experiment
CENTRAL

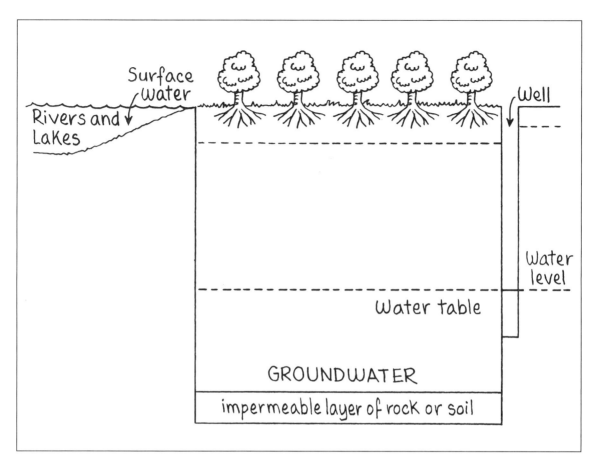

Surface water — Rivers and Lakes, Well, Water level, Water table, GROUNDWATER, impermeable layer of rock or soil

Our most precious resource?

Water is a natural but limited resource. Most of the water on Earth is saltwater; 97 percent of the world's water supply is located in the oceans. That means that only 3 percent is freshwater, and two-thirds of that is frozen in the polar icecaps, icebergs, and glaciers. Only the remaining 1 percent is groundwater or **surface water** in lakes, ponds, and streams.

Today, about three-quarters of the cities in the United States depend on groundwater for part or all of their drinking water. Wells also withdraw groundwater to irrigate crops, keep golf courses green, and meet other recreational needs.

When water is pumped out of an aquifer into a well, the water level drops. If rainfall does not replace that water, the aquifer becomes overdrawn. When water is pumped out faster than it is replaced, the ground may sink, creating sinkholes.

Where groundwater occurs.

(**Words to Know**

Impurities:
Chemicals or other pollutants in water.

Nonpoint source:
An unidentified source of pollution, which may actually be a number of sources.

Percolate:
To pass through a permeable substance.

Permeable:
Having pores that permit a liquid or a gas to pass through.

experiment
CENTRAL

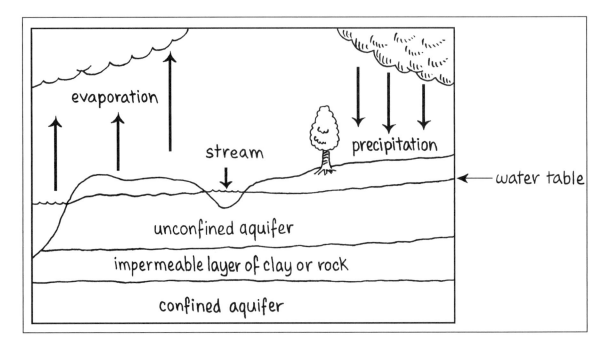

evaporation

stream

precipitation

water table

unconfined aquifer

impermeable layer of clay or rock

confined aquifer

Confined and unconfined aquifers.

Can aquifers become polluted?

Contamination is another problem. Leaking underground storage tanks may seep petroleum products into groundwater. Inadequate septic systems, sewage treatment plants, fertilizer runoff from farms, salt runoff from highways, and chemicals discharged from factories are other sources of pollution that can make groundwater unsuitable for humans to drink or use.

Pollution can come from specific, identified locations, called **point sources,** or from scattered areas, called **nonpoint sources.** Most groundwater pollution comes from nonpoint sources. Once an aquifer is polluted, it may remain that way for years.

Wetlands provide homes for waterfowl and many other animal species. Low-lying wetlands may receive water from an aquifer. If the water is contaminated, it will pollute the wetlands, affecting all the wildlife that depends on these water habitats.

As the human population continues to grow, the demand for fresh, clean water supplies grows too. Careful management and use are essential to maintain the quality of our groundwater and surface water. The following projects will help you understand how aquifers can become contaminated and how dirty water can be cleaned.

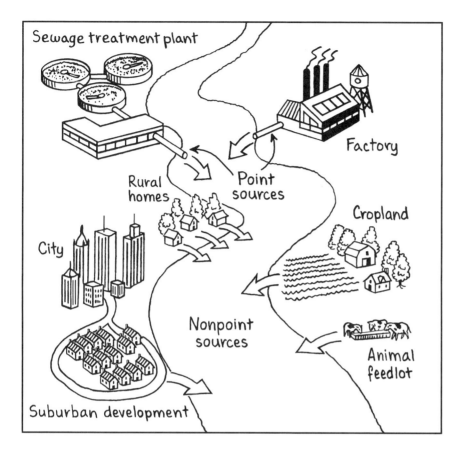

Sources of water pollution.

Project 1
Aquifers: How do they become polluted?

Purpose

Many communities and homeowners must rely on wells that pump groundwater from aquifers. Unfortunately, groundwater can be contaminated by improper use or disposal of harmful chemicals, such as lawn fertilizers and household cleaners. These chemicals can percolate down through the soil and rock into an aquifer and eventually be drawn into the wells. Such contamination can pose a significant threat to human health.

In this project, you will build a model that shows how water is stored in an aquifer, how groundwater can become contaminated, and how this contamination can end up in a well. You will see that what

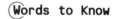

Words to Know

Unconfined aquifer:
An aquifer under a layer of permeable rock and soil.

Variable:
Something that can affect the results of an experiment.

Water table:
The level of the upper surface of groundwater.

Wetlands:
Areas that are wet or covered with water for at least part of the year.

happens above ground can affect the aquifers below ground—and the drinking water.

Level of Difficulty

Moderate, because of the time involved.

Materials Needed

- 6x8-inch (15x20-centimeter) clear plastic container at least 6 inches (15 centimeters) deep
- 1 pound (.45 kilogram) modeling clay
- 2 pounds (.9 kilograms) play sand
- 2 pounds (.9 kilograms) aquarium gravel or pebbles, rinsed
- plastic drinking straw
- plastic spray bottle with a clear spray stem
- green felt, 3x5 inches (7.6x12.7 centimeters)
- 0.25 cup (59 milliliters) powdered cocoa
- red food coloring
- clean water
- tape

experiment
CENTRAL

Approximate Budget

$10 to $20 for the container, sand, clay, spray bottle, and other materials.

Timetable

1 to 2 hours.

Step-by-Step Instructions

1. Tape the straw vertically inside the plastic container along one side, as illustrated on page 314. Do not let the bottom end of the straw touch the bottom of the container. This will be the "well."

2. Pour a 1.5-inch (3.8-centimeter) layer of sand on the bottom of the container.

3. Pour water into the sand, wetting it completely without creating puddles. The water will be absorbed into the sand, surrounding the particles, much as it is stored in an aquifer.

Pollution in groundwater aquifers can harm the wildlife in wetlands. (Peter Arnold Inc. Reproduced by permission.)

How to Work Safely

Do not drink the water you are using in this project.

4. Flatten the clay into a thin layer and cover half the sand with it, pressing the clay into three sides of the container. The clay represents the confining or impermeable layer that keeps water from passing through.

5. Pour a small amount of water onto the clay. Most should remain on top of the clay, with some flowing into the uncovered sand.

6. Cover the whole surface of the sand and clay with the aquarium rocks. On one side, slope the rocks to form a hill and a valley.

Steps 1 to 7 : How to build an aquifer.

7. Fill the container with water until it is nearly even with the top of your hill. See how the water is stored around the rocks in the aquifer. Also notice a surface supply of water (a small lake). This model represents groundwater and surface water, both of which can be used for drinking.

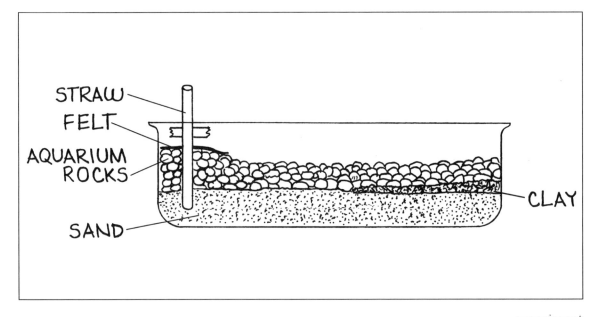

experiment
CENTRAL

8. Put a few drops of red food coloring into the straw to represent pollution. People often use old wells to dispose of farm chemicals, trash, and used motor oils. The food coloring will color the sand. This demonstrates one way that pollution can spread into and through an aquifer.

9. Place the green felt on the hill. Use a little clay to fasten it to the sides of the container.

10. Sprinkle some cocoa on the hill, representing the improper use of materials such as lawn chemicals or fertilizers.

11. Fill the spray bottle with water. Make it rain on the hill and over the aquifer. The cocoa will seep through the felt and wash into the surface water. This is another way that pollution reaches aquifers.

12. Check the area around the straw. The pollution has probably spread farther. Remove the top of the spray bottle and insert the stem into the straw. Depress the trigger to pull up water from the well. Note its appearance. This is the same water that people would drink. It also is contaminated.

Summary of Results

From your model, you can easily see how pollution spread into the surface water and the aquifer, contaminating the water supply. Write a paragraph about what you observed.

Troubleshooter's Guide

Here is a problem that might arise, a possible cause, and a way to remedy the problem.

Problem: The straw is clogged with sand.

Possible cause: The straw is too close to the bottom of the container. Make sure you put the straw in first and leave a small space between it and the bottom of the container. Then pour in the sand. If sand still clogs the straw, gently blow through the straw to unclog it.

Project 2
Groundwater: How can it be cleaned?

Purpose

Surface water—water in lakes, rivers, and wetlands—often contains **impurities** that make it look and smell bad. It may also contain bacteria and other organisms that can cause disease. Consequently, this water must be "cleaned" before it can be used. Water treatment plants typically clean water by taking it through these processes:

- **aeration,** which allows foul-smelling gases to escape and adds oxygen from the air
- **coagulation,** which causes solid particles to stick together
- **sedimentation,** which allows gravity to pull the solid particles out of a liquid
- **filtration,** which removes more impurities with a filter
- **disinfection,** which uses chemicals to kill harmful organisms

This project will demonstrate the procedures that municipal water plants use to purify water. It's important to maintain a clean water supply, as this water often affects the quality of the groundwater used by people who depend on wells.

Level of Difficulty

Moderate.

Materials Needed

- 10.5 pints (5 liters) of "swamp water" (or add 2.5 cups of dirt or mud to 10.5 pints of water)
- 3 large clear plastic soft-drink bottles: 1 with a cap; 1 with its top removed; 1 with its bottom removed
- 1.5-quart (1.5-liter) or larger beaker (or another clear plastic soft-drink bottle bottom)
- 2 tablespoons (20 grams) alum (potassium aluminum sulfate; available from biological supply houses or ask your teacher for a source.)
- 1.5 pounds (0.7 kilograms) fine sand
- 1.5 pounds (0.7 kilograms) coarse sand
- 1 pound (0.5 kilograms) small pebbles (natural color aquarium rocks, washed)

experiment
CENTRAL

- large (500 milliliter or larger) beaker or jar
- coffee filter
- rubber band
- stirrer
- scissors

Approximate Budget

$10 for sand, pebbles, and alum.

Timetable

1 to 2 hours.

Step-by-Step Instructions

1. Pour about 1.5 quart (1.5 liter) of the swamp water into the uncut soft-drink bottle. On a data sheet, describe the look and smell of the water.

2. To aerate the water, place the cap on the bottle and shake it vigorously for 30 seconds. The shaking allows gases trapped in the water to escape and adds oxygen to the water. Then pour the water back and forth between the bottle with the cap and the cut-off bottle ten times. Describe any changes in the water. Pour the aerated water into the large beaker or bottle bottom.

3. To coagulate solid impurities in the water so they can be removed, add the alum crystals to the water. Slowly stir for 5 minutes.

4. To allow sedimentation, let the water stand undisturbed for 20 minutes. Observe it at 5-minute intervals and write your observations about the changes in the water's appearance.

5. Construct a filter from the bottle with its bottom removed. First, attach the coffee filter to the outside of the neck of the bottle with a rubber band. Turn the bottle top upside down and pour in a layer of pebbles. The filter will prevent the pebbles from falling out.

 ## How to Work Safely

Do not drink the water you are using in this project. Be careful using the scissors when you cut the tops and bottoms off the soda bottles.

Step 5: Constructing a water filter.

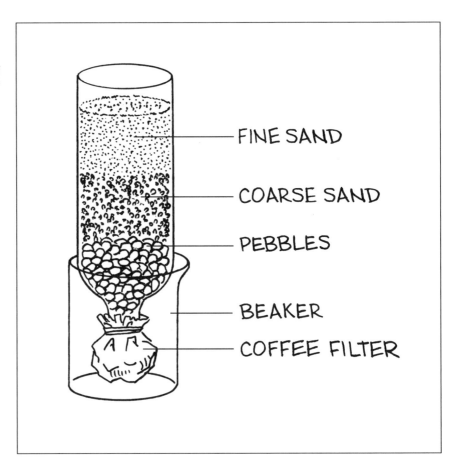

FINE SAND

COARSE SAND

PEBBLES

BEAKER

COFFEE FILTER

Pour the coarse sand on top of the pebbles. Pour the fine sand on top of the coarse sand. Clean the filter by slowly and carefully pouring through 10.5 pints (5 liters), or more, of clean tap water. Try not to disturb the top layer of sand as you pour.

6. To filter the swamp water, wait until a large amount of sediment has settled on the bottom of the bottle of swamp water. Then carefully—without disturbing the sediment—pour the top two-thirds of the swamp water through the filter. Collect the filtered water in a beaker or other container.

7. Compare the smell and appearance of the treated and untreated water.

Note: The final step in water treatment is disinfection by adding chemicals to kill any harmful organisms. Because disinfectants must be handled carefully, this process is not included here. Do remember that the water you have treated is NOT safe to drink.

experiment
CENTRAL

Troubleshooter's Guide

Here is a problem that might arise during this project, a possible cause, and a way to remedy the problem.

Problem: During sedimentation, the sediments mixed into the water that was being filtered.

Possible cause: You might have poured the swamp water too quickly. Pour the contaminated water back into the sedimentation bottle and let it sit undisturbed again. Or pour it through the coffee filter and see if the sediment makes the water flow more slowly. The filter may not take all the sediment out, or it may become clogged with sediment, one of the many problems that occur during the actual water treatment process.

Summary of Results

Write a report of your observations of the smell and look of the water before and after treatment. Include the amount of time that it took for the sediments to form.

 Design Your Own Experiment

How to Select a Topic Relating to this Concept

You have seen how water enters an aquifer, how it flows from the aquifer into wetlands, and how it is drawn into wells. Perhaps you wonder how long it takes to replenish the supply of groundwater that is removed from the aquifer. You can use the aquifer you built in Project 1 to design your own experiment to determine how long it takes to replace the water that is removed.

Check the For More Information section and talk with your science teacher or school or community media specialist to start gathering information on groundwater questions that interest you. As you consider possible experiments, be sure to discuss them with a knowledgeable adult before trying them.

Where does your drinking water come from? (Photo Researchers Inc. Reproduced by permission.)

Steps in the Scientific Method

To do an original experiment, you need to plan carefully and think things through. Otherwise, you might not be sure what question you are answering, what you are or should be measuring, or what your findings prove or disprove.

Here are the steps in designing an experiment:

- State the purpose of—and the underlying question behind—the experiment you propose to do.
- Recognize the variables involved, and select one that will help you answer the question at hand.
- State a testable hypothesis, an educated guess about the answer to your question.
- Decide how to change the **variable** you selected
- Decide how to measure your results.

Recording Data and Summarizing the Results

In the two groundwater projects, the results were not measurable. However, in designing your own experiment, you should decide how to record the data, how to measure much water you draw out, and how to determine how quickly the same amount of water is replenished.

Related Projects

You can undertake a variety of projects related to groundwater, such as finding out the source(s) of drinking water in your community and what steps are being taken to prevent contamination. You might research the kinds of contaminants found most often in your community's water and the probable sources of these contaminants. You might explore how flooding and drought each affect groundwater and its purity. If possible, compare the smell and appearance of surface water

experiment
CENTRAL

and groundwater—or water that has been treated by the city water division and water from a well. The possibilities just depend on your interests.

For More Information

Dobson, Clive, and Gregor Gilpin Beck. *Watersheds: A Practical Handbook for Healthy Water.* Buffalo, NY: Firefly Books, 1999. ❖ Provides an overview of the fundamentals of ecology and the web of life through the water cycle.

Kellert, Stephen, general editor. *MacMillan Encyclopedia of the Environment.* New York: Simon and Schuster, 1997. ❖ Provides information on the water cycle and related topics.

U.S. Environmental Protection Agency Web Site. www.epa.gov/seahome/groundwater ❖ Provides information on groundwater aquifers and projects and activities that help explain the water cycle and aquifers.

VanCleave, Janice. *Janice VanCleave's Ecology for Every Kid.* New York: John Wiley & Sons, 1996. ❖ Provides projects and information on the water cycle and water pollution.

chapter 22

Heat

Your feet are bare, and the Sun has been beating down on the sidewalk outside your home all day. You form a **hypothesis** or educated guess that the sidewalk is cool enough to allow you to walk on it without burning your feet. You decide to test your hypothesis, knowing that if you are wrong, you could be in for some painful moments!

But how does heat from the sidewalk burn your feet? **Heat** is a form of energy produced by the motion of molecules that make up a substance. The faster the molecules move, the more heat they produce and the higher the temperature of the sidewalk or other substance. **Temperature** is the measure of the average energy of the molecules in a substance. Heat can travel from one body to another in three ways: by conduction, by convection, and by radiation.

What is conduction?

Conduction is the flow of heat through a solid. When you walk on a hot sidewalk, the concrete warms—or burns—your feet through conduction. When a warmer substance with quickly moving molecules (the sidewalk) comes into contact with a cooler substance with slowly moving molecules (your bare feet), the faster molecules bump into the slower ones and make them move faster, too.

As the slower molecules pick up speed, the cooler substance gets warmer. The warmer substance loses some of its heat energy and gets cooler. **Heat energy** is the energy produced when two substances that have different temperatures are combined. The greater the difference in temperatures, the faster both temperatures change.

Words to Know

Conduction:
The flow of heat through a solid.

Control experiment:
A setup that is identical to the experiment but is not affected by the variable that will be changed during the experiment.

Convection:
The circulatory motion that occurs in a gas or liquid at a nonuniform temperature owing to the variation of its density and the action of gravity.

The quickly vibrating molecules in the hot sidewalk can transfer their heat energy to your cool feet. (Richard B. Levine. Reproduced by permission.)

ⓦords to Know

Convection current:
A circular movement of a fluid in response to alternating heating and cooling.

Electromagnetic waves:
Radiation that has properties of both an electric and a magnetic wave and that travels through a vacuum with the speed of light.

Greenhouse effect:
The warming of Earth's atmosphere due to water vapor, carbon dioxide, and other gases in the atmosphere that trap heat radiated from Earth's surface.

Heat:
A form of energy produced by the motion of molecules that make up a substance.

Heat energy:
The energy produced when two substances that have different temperatures are combined.

experiment
CENTRAL

A burner heats the air inside the balloon. As the hot air rises into the cooler atmosphere, the balloon rises, too. (Photo Researchers Inc. Reproduced by permission.)

Some substances conduct or transfer heat better than others. In Experiment 1, you will test five substances to see which is the best conductor of heat.

What is convection?

The second way heat travels is by convection. **Convection** is the rising of warm air from an object, such as the surface of Earth. Convection allows heat to travel through both gases and liquids, moving from warmer areas to cooler areas.

Heating the molecules in a gas or liquid makes them move farther apart, so the substance becomes lighter or less dense. The lighter air or liquid rises; it also cools off as heat energy escapes into the surrounding cooler air or liquid. As the molecules cool, they move closer together, and the substance becomes heavier or more dense and falls again.

experiment
CENTRAL

As warm air rises over land, convection causes cool air from the ocean to rush in and take its place. The result is wind. (Photo Researchers Inc. Reproduced by permission.)

In Experiment 2, you will use colored water to create convection currents that show how heat moves through a liquid. A **convection current** is a circular movement of a fluid in response to alternating heating and cooling.

What is radiation?

Radiation is energy transmitted in the form of **electromagnetic waves** that travel through the vacuum of space at the speed of light. **Infrared radiation** consists of wavelengths that are shorter than **radio waves** but longer than visible light. Infrared radiation takes the form of heat. These heat rays are much like light rays except that we cannot see them.

That hot sidewalk was heated by infrared radiation from the Sun. The Sun's heat did not travel to the sidewalk by conduction or convection because the Sun and sidewalk are separated by the vacuum of space. The transfer of heat by radiation does not require that the hotter and cooler substances touch each other.

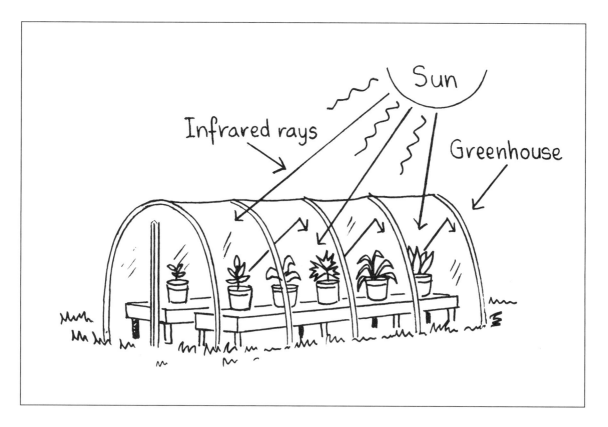

Not only the Sun, but all hot objects give out infrared radiation. This radiation gives up its heat energy when it is absorbed by an object, but this energy can also be reflected back toward its source. If that sidewalk had been painted white, it would have reflected the Sun's radiation, just as white clothing does. Why? The color white does not absorb light; it reflects it. Dark colors absorb light—and heat.

The more you know about ways that heat travels, the better able you will be to use heat to your advantage and not be at its mercy.

Sunlight passes through the glass and heats the plants. The warm plants give off infrared radiation, but these rays are longer and cannot pass back through the glass. Trapped inside the greenhouse, the rays heat the air. Pollution in the atmosphere can trap heat close to Earth in the same way. This is called the greenhouse effect.

Experiment 1
Conduction: Which solid materials are the best conductors of heat?

Purpose/Hypothesis

In this experiment, you will test short lengths of five different materials to compare their ability to conduct heat. Each length will have a dab of wax on one end holding a bead in place. You will heat the oppo-

What Are the Variables?

Variables are anything that might affect the results of an experiment. Here are the main variables in this experiment:

- the types of conducting materials

- the air temperature during the experiment

- the amount of each conducting material that comes into contact with the water

- the temperature of the water

- the type of wax used

- the amount of wax placed on the end of each conducting material

- the size and type of beads

In other words, the variables in this experiment are everything that might affect the time it takes for each bit of wax to release its bead. If you change more than one variable, you will not be able to tell which variable had the most effect on the rate at which the wax melted.

site end of the lengths with hot water. The time it takes for each bit of wax to melt and release its bead will tell you which material conducted heat the fastest. Before you begin, make an educated guess about the outcome of this experiment based on your knowledge of heat. This educated guess, or prediction, is your **hypothesis.** A hypothesis should explain these things:

- the topic of the experiment
- the variable you will change
- the variable you will measure
- what you expect to happen

A hypothesis should be brief, specific, and measurable. It must be something you can test through observation. Your experiment will prove or disprove whether your hypothesis is correct. Here is one possible hypothesis for this experiment: "Copper will conduct heat faster than the four other materials; wood will be the slowest conductor."

In this case, the **variables** you will change are the conducting materials, and the variable you will measure is the time it takes each bit of wax to melt and release its bead. You expect the wax on the copper length to melt first, and the wax on the wood to melt last or not at all.

You will also set up a **control experiment** to make sure that it is conducted heat from the water and not some other variable that melts the wax. To set up the control experiment, you will create an additional set of the five conducting materials, attach wax and beads to the ends, but not heat them. If the wax melts off the experimental copper length first and the experimental wood length last and if no wax melts off the control materials, you will know your hypothesis is correct.

Level of Difficulty

Moderate/high, because of safety factors; ask an adult to help you complete this experiment.

Materials Needed

- two 4-inch (10-centimeter) lengths of these materials:
  18-gauge copper wire
  18-gauge aluminum wire
  18-gauge steel wire
- glass stirrer or solid glass rod
- 0.13-inch (0.3-centimeter) diameter wooden dowel
- 10 identical beads (glass or plastic)
- candle
- matches
- 2 glass bowls (with straight sides, if possible)
- very hot tap water
- clay
- stop watch or clock with a second hand

How to Experiment Safely

Be sure to ask an adult to help you with this experiment. Handle the matches, lighted candle, and hot water carefully to avoid burns. Keep your clothing away from the flame. Dripping wax can also cause burns.

Approximate Budget

$4 for the wire, glass stirrer, dowel, and beads. The other materials should be available in most households.

Timetable

30 minutes to set up and conduct the experiment.

Step-by-Step Instructions

1. Use a match to light the candle. Then follow this procedure for each of the five conducting materials:

   a. Have your adult helper drip one drop of wax on one end of the conducting material.

   b. Quickly push a bead into the drop of wax and make sure it is securely lodged there.

   c. Use a piece of clay to attach the conducting material to the side of one bowl, as illustrated. Space the conducting materials even-ly around the bowl and anchor them firmly with the clay so they will remain upright. Make sure each material extends the same distance into the bowl.

2. Repeat Step 1 to set up the control experiment in the second glass bowl.

LEFT: Step 1: Have an adult helper drip one drop of wax on one end of the conducting material.

RIGHT: Step 1C: Use a piece of clay to attach the conducting material to the side of one bowl. Space the conducting materials even-ly around the bowl and anchor them firmly with the clay so they will remain upright.

experiment
CENTRAL

3. Ask the adult to carefully pour about 2 inches (5 centimeters) of very hot tap water into the center of the experimental bowl. As the water level rises, it should touch the lower end of each conducting material. Make sure each material extends the same distance into the water.

4. Immediately start the stop watch. Record on a chart (see page 332) how long it takes for each bead to fall from its conducting material.

5. Observe the beads in your control experiment and record on the chart their position at the end of the experiment.

Summary of Results

Use the data on your chart to create a line graph of your findings. The graph will indicate the time that lapsed before each bead fell. Then study your chart and graph and decide whether your hypothesis was correct. Did the bead on the experimental copper wire fall first, and the one on the wooden dowel fall last or not at all? Did the beads in the control experiment remain in place? Write a paragraph summarizing your findings and explaining whether they support your hypothesis.

For your reference, here is a list of the materials in the experiment, plus a few more, with a number that represents their ability to conduct heat, called **thermal conductivity**. The higher the number, the better the material conducts heat.

Silver	58.2
Copper	55.2
Aluminum	29.4
Steel	7.2
Glass	0.12
Wood	0.012
Air	0.004
Styrofoam	0.0034

Change the Variables

You can conduct similar experiments by changing the variables. For example, you can use other conducting materials, such as plastic, iron, or a stick of insulating foam. You can also place a different small object in the wax, such as a metal nail.

Chart of Responses

Experimental conductors	Time taken for bead to fall
Copper wire	
Aluminum wire	
Steel wire	
Glass rod	
Wooden dowel	

Control conductors	Position of bead at end of experiment
Copper wire	
Aluminum wire	
Steel wire	
Glass rod	
Wooden dowel	

Troubleshooter's Guide

Here are some problems that may arise during this experiment, some possible causes, and ways to remedy the problems.

Problem: The bead on a different conductor fell before the bead on the copper conductor.

Possible causes:

1. The hot water might have splashed against the conductors as you poured it, giving some conductors a head start in transferring heat. Try again, pouring slowly.

2. Some conductors may have more wax than the others, affecting the melting speed. Try again, making sure to drip the same amount of wax on all conductors.

Problem: A conductor other than the wooden dowel was the last one to release its bead.

Possible cause: See possible cause 2 above.

Problem: A bead on a control conductor fell off, or most of the beads fell off immediately.

Possible causes:

1. The beads are too large or heavy. Try again with smaller, lighter beads.

2. The beads were not firmly attached. Try again, pushing the beads firmly into the wax.

3. The room air temperature is too warm, helping to melt the wax. Move to a cooler location or repeat your experiment on a cooler day.

Another way to measure conductivity is to use small containers made of different materials, such as a glass jar, an insulated cup, a plastic cup, and a steel can. Put an ice cube in each small container and place them all in a larger container holding a few inches of very hot water. To determine the best conductor, record how long it takes for the ice to melt in each small container.

OPPOSITE PAGE:
Steps 4 and 5: Recording chart for Experiment 1.

Experiment 2
Convection: How does heat move through liquids?

Purpose/Hypothesis
In this experiment, you will put tinted hot water into cold water and tinted cold water into hot water. In both cases, you will observe and record the movement of the water to determine how heat moves through liquids. Your experiment should cause convection currents to develop as heat moves through the water. Before you begin, make an educated guess about the outcome of this experiment based on your knowledge of heat. This educated guess, or prediction, is your **hypothesis.** A hypothesis should explain these things:

- the topic of the experiment
- the variable you will change
- the variable you will measure
- what you expect to happen

A hypothesis should be brief, specific, and measurable. It must be something you can test through observation. Your experiment will

What Are the Variables?
Variables are anything that might affect the results of an experiment. Here are the main variables in this experiment:

- the temperatures of the water in different containers

- the amount of water being dropped into water of a different temperature

- whether the containers of water are stirred or otherwise disturbed

In other words, the variables in this experiment are everything that might affect the motion of the tinted water. If you change more than one variable, you will not be able to tell which one had the most effect on the movement of the water.

experiment
CENTRAL

prove or disprove whether your hypothesis is correct. Here is a possible hypothesis for this experiment: "Hot water placed in cold water will rise, and cold water placed in hot water will fall."

In this case, the **variable** you will change is the temperature of the tinted water placed in the container and the water already in the container, and the variable you will measure is the motion of the tinted water. You expect the cold blue water will sink and the hot red water will rise.

As a **control experiment**, you will also pour tinted room-temperature water into more room-temperature water to determine if it, too, moves in a certain pattern. During your experiment, if the hot water rises, the cold water falls, and the room-temperature water mixes together in no specific pattern, you will know your hypothesis is correct.

Level of Difficulty
Easy/moderate.

Materials Needed
- 1 small container of very hot water, tinted red with food coloring
- 1 large container of very hot water
- 1 small container of icy cold water, tinted blue
- 1 large container of icy cold water
- 1 small container of room-temperature water, tinted green
- 1 large container of room-temperature water
- 2 eye droppers

Approximate Budget
Less than $5 for food coloring and eye droppers.

Timetable
20 minutes.

 ## How to Experiment Safely
Handle the hot water carefully to avoid burns. You might ask an adult to help you put the hot water into the containers.

RIGHT: Step 1: Using one eye dropper, add 2 drops of the red (hot) water to the large container of cold water.

BELOW: Steps 1 to 3: Recording chart for Experiment 2.

Step-by-Step Instructions

1. Using one eye dropper, add 2 drops of the red (hot) water to the large container of cold water. Observe and record the movement of the red water on a chart similar to the one illustrated. DO NOT STIR OR BUMP THE LARGE CONTAINER. Rinse the eye dropper.

2. Using the other eye dropper, add 2 drops

Heat Movement

Instructions: Draw your large container and use arrows to show direction of the water's movement.

Red (hot) water in cold water:

Blue (cold) water in hot water:

Green (room-temperature) water in room-temperature water:

experiment
CENTRAL

of the blue (cold) water to the large container of hot water. Record the movement of the blue water on the chart. AGAIN, DO NOT STIR OR BUMP THE LARGE CONTAINER.

3. As a control experiment, use the rinsed, room-temperature eye dropper to add 2 drops of green (room-temperature) water to the large container of room-temperature water. Record what happens.

Summary of Results

Study the drawings on your chart and decide whether your hypothesis was correct. Did the hot water rise, the cold water fall, and the room-temperature water mix in no specific pattern? Write a paragraph summarizing your findings and explaining whether they support your hypothesis.

Change the Variables

Change the way that water of a different temperature is introduced: immerse a glass tube that is open on both ends in a container of very warm (not burning) water colored red. Put your finger over the top of

Troubleshooter's Guide

Here are some problems that may arise during this experiment, some possible causes, and ways to remedy the problems.

Problem: The tinted hot water (or the tinted cold water) simply spread throughout the water in the experimental large container, in no particular pattern.

Possible cause: The difference between the water temperatures was too small. Make sure the cold water is icy and the hot water is very hot. Heat water in a microwave for a minute, if you wish, but ask an adult to help you handle it, using pot holders. Use containers that are microwave-safe.

Problem: You could not clearly see the movement of the hot (or cold) water in the large container.

Possible cause: The water was not tinted dark enough. Add more food coloring and try again.

the tube, which should stop the water from flowing out either end. Now immerse the tube in a container of icy cold water. Hold the tube in a vertical position and take your finger off the end of the tube. Observe whether the red water flows out of the top or the bottom of the tube. Try the same experiment with cold, blue water in the tube and very warm water in the large container. From which end of the tube does the blue water flow?

 # Design Your Own Experiment

How to Select a Topic Relating to this Concept

You can explore many other aspects of heat movement. For example, you might investigate the relationship between convection and wind, or you could find out how surface area affects the rate of heat conduction. For example, does water boil more quickly if it is in a wide pan or a narrow pan? Does ice melt more quickly if it is crushed into small pieces?

Check the For More Information section and talk with your science teacher or school or community media specialist to start gathering information on heat questions that interest you. As you consider possible experiments, be sure to discuss them with your science teacher or another knowledgeable adult before trying them. Experimenting with heat is potentially dangerous.

Steps in the Scientific Method

To do an original experiment, you need to plan carefully and think things through. Otherwise, you might not be sure what question you are answering, what you are or should be measuring, or what your findings prove or disprove.

Here are the steps in designing an experiment:

- State the purpose of—and the underlying question behind—the experiment you propose to do.
- Recognize the variables involved, and select one that will help you answer the question at hand.
- State a testable hypothesis, an educated guess about the answer to your question.
- Decide how to change the variable you selected.
- Decide how to measure your results.

experiment

Recording Data and Summarizing the Results

In the heat movement experiments, your raw data might include charts, graphs, drawings, and photographs of the changes you observed. If you display your experiment, make clear your beginning question, the variable you changed, the variable you measured, the results, and your conclusions. Explain what materials you used, how long each step took, and other basic information.

Related Projects

You can undertake a variety of projects related to the movement of heat. For example, you might explore which kinds of home insulation, insulated cups, or insulated gloves are most efficient at stopping the movement of heat through conduction. When a fireplace burns, how much of the heat escapes up the chimney through convection? Which colors are most efficient at reflecting radiated heat?

For More Information

Friedhoffer, Robert. *Molecules and Heat.* New York: Franklin Watts, 1992. ❖ Explores scientific concepts involving heat and heat movement by turning them into "magic tricks."

Garner, Robert, and Eric Kemer. *Science Projects about Temperature and Heat.* Hillside, NJ: Enslow Publishers, 1994. ❖ Provides detailed explanations of projects and the concepts they demonstrate.

Gutnik, Martin. *Experiments That Explore the Greenhouse Effect.* Brookfield, CT: Millbrook Press, 1991. ❖ Outlines experiments that relate to the movement of heat as it causes the greenhouse effect.

Wood, Robert. *Heat FUNdamentals.* New York: Learning Triangle Press, 1997. ❖ Offers more than 25 heat-related activities and brief explanations.

chapter 23

Life Cycles

All animals go through changes during their lives. Some simply grow larger, while others completely change their forms. This kind of change is called **metamorphosis,** which means "change in form."

Some insects have no metamorphosis, simply growing larger and becoming able to reproduce. Others undergo an **incomplete metamorphosis,** in which the immature insects are known as **nymphs.** Nymphs, which often live in water, resemble the adult forms, but their wings are not fully developed and they have no reproductive organs. Nymphs gradually become adults by **molting,** or shedding their outermost layer.

Other insects go through a **complete mctamorphosis,** in which the immature stage is called a **larva.** Caterpillars, for example, are the larvae of butterflies. The larva becomes a **pupa,** which is mostly a resting stage. Finally, the pupa emerges as a full-fledged adult, such as a

Words to Know

Amphibians:
Animals that live on land and breathe air but return to the water to reproduce.

Complete metamorphosis:
Metamorphosis in which a larva becomes a pupa before changing into an adult form.

A caterpillar represents the larvae stage in a complete metamorphosis. (Photo Researchers Inc. Reproduced by permission.)

The butterfly is the adult stage in the life cycle that begins as a caterpillar. (Peter Arnold Inc. Reproduced by permission.)

butterfly. Organisms in different stages of the life cycle often live in different habitats and eat different foods.

What other organisms go through metamorphosis?

Amphibians also go through a dramatic metamorphosis. You are probably familiar with the life cycle of the frog, which begins with a tadpole. You may have seen tadpoles in a pond or stream. An aquatic animal with a tail, the tadpole not only grows as it gets older, it also changes its form, growing legs, living at least partly on land, and losing its tail. While tadpoles eat tiny aquatic vegetation, adult frogs eat just about any small animal that flies, jumps, or crawls past and can fit in their mouths.

Why should we learn about metamorphosis?

Many people are interested in the life cycles of animals. Farmers must know about insect life cycles in order to control harmful insects and

A "froglet" is one stage in the frog's life cycle. (Photo Researchers Inc. Reproduced by permission.)

encourage the helpful ones that help pollinate their plants, such as bees and butterflies. **Ecologists** are also interested in metamorphosis. Many amphibians are threatened with extinction due to the destruction of their habitat. Ecologists study metamorphosis to learn the needs of different stages of amphibian life cycles and better understand how to save them.

What questions do you have about life cycles? You will have an opportunity to explore life cycles in the following experiments. You will learn more about this natural phenomenon that can be so fascinating and dramatic to observe.

Experiment 1
Tadpoles: Does temperature affect the rate at which tadpoles change into frogs?

Purpose/Hypothesis

WARNING: *Do not perform this experiment unless you have a safe, approved spot to release live frogs once experiment is completed. You should be aware that it is illegal to release or dispose of live frogs in certain areas. If you are not sure about performing this experiment, ask your science teacher.*

In this experiment, you will discover how the water temperature in which tadpoles live affects how fast they grow and become adult frogs. Tadpoles are the larval form of frogs. They hatch from eggs laid by a female frog. Tadpoles live in the water and breathe through gills, but when they become frogs or toads, they breathe air and live mostly on land. Tadpoles eat only plants, while adult frogs eat insects and even small snakes. Before you begin, make an educated guess about the outcome of this experiment based on your knowledge of tadpoles. This educated guess, or prediction, is your **hypothesis.** A hypothesis should explain these things:

- the topic of the experiment
- the variable you will change
- the variable you will measure
- what you expect to happen

A hypothesis should be brief, specific, and measurable. It must be something you can test through observation. Your experiment will prove or disprove your hypothesis. Here is one possible hypothesis for this experiment: "The higher the water temperature, the faster tadpoles will become frogs."

What Are the Variables?

Variables are anything that might affect the results of an experiment. Here are the main variables in this experiment:

- the temperature of the water

- the number of tadpoles in each bucket

- the age, size, and health of the tadpoles in each bucket

- the tadpoles' diet

In other words, the variables in this experiment are everything that might affect the time it takes for the tadpoles to become frogs. If you change more than one variable, you will not be able to tell which variable had the most effect on the time for the tadpoles to metamorphose.

In this case, the **variable** you will change will be the temperature of the water, and the variable you will measure will be the number of days it takes for the tadpoles to become frogs. You expect the tadpoles in the warmest water to develop into frogs first.

Setting up a **control experiment** will help you isolate one variable. Only one variable will change between the control and the experimental buckets, and that is the temperature of the water. For the control, you will use water at the air temperature outside (or at room temperature if your region is experiencing winter now). For the experimental buckets, you will have warmer and cooler water.

You will measure the number of days it takes the tadpoles to become adult frogs. You will know they are fully adult when they completely lose their tails and have fully developed legs. If warmer water results in a faster metamorphosis, your hypothesis is correct.

Level of Difficulty
Difficult, because of care required with live animals.

Materials Needed
- 5 buckets or large glass jars with lids
- water to fill the containers (Allow it to sit at least overnight to let any chlorine in it evaporate.)
- a steady supply of boiled lettuce
- 5 thermometers
- large aquarium fish net

How to Experiment Safely

Be careful when handling live animals, and treat them with respect and care. Avoid touching the tadpoles because amphibians have extremely sensitive skin. Wash your hands before and after you touch the water. If you decide to find your own tadpoles in a pond or stream, ask an adult to help you. You should be aware that it is illegal to release or dispose of live frogs in certain areas. If you are not sure about performing this experiment, ask your science teacher.

- about 25 tadpoles (You can order tadpoles from a biological supply company, such as those listed in the For More Information section, or you might find them in a stream or pond.)

Approximate Budget
$30 for thermometers and tadpoles.

Timetable
About 4 weeks.

Step-by-Step Instructions

1. Fill each of the five containers with the same amount of water. Add a thermometer to each container.

2. Use the net to place five tadpoles in each container.

3. Place each container so that the water temperatures will be different. Leave one at room temperature. Place one outside as your control. Place another under a lamp that will be left on constantly. Place one container in a cool, dark place, such as under a counter. Put the last one in the refrigerator. (Tadpoles in the wild often live in quite cold water.)

Steps 1 and 2: Fill the five containers each with the same amount of water. Place five tadpoles in each container.

4. After an hour, record the water temperature in each container on a data sheet similar to the one illustrated.

Container	Temperature	Days to metamorphosis
1		
2		
3		
4		
5		

Container	Day (record size each day)							
	1	2	3	4	5	6	7	8...
1								
2								
3								
4								
5								

Step 4: Recording chart for Experiment 1.

5. Feed all your tadpoles about a silver-dollar-sized piece of boiled lettuce every day or every other day. Do not overfeed because the lettuce will rot. Record how much food you put in the containers each day.

6. Change the water regularly, perhaps every other day. Use water that has been allowed to sit overnight and is at the same temperature as the water you are replacing. Putting tadpoles in water that

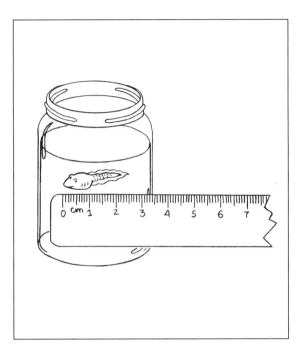

Step 7: Measure the size of the tadpoles in each container every week.

is much warmer or cooler than they are used to could kill them. If any tadpoles die for any reason, remove them as soon as possible.

7. Record the water temperature in each container each day, and describe each group of tadpoles. You may want to sketch them. Measure their size each week and record it on your data sheet.

8. After a group of tadpoles becomes frogs, which could take several weeks, record the number of days and release them into an area where it is safe and legal to do so.

You should be aware that it is illegal to release or dispose of live frogs in certain areas. If you are not sure about where to release your frogs, ask your science teacher.

9. Continue making observations and recording data until all the tadpoles have become frogs.

Summary of Results

Study the results on your chart. How many days did it take for the first group to become frogs? What was the water temperature in that container? Did tadpoles in cooler containers take longer to go through metamorphosis? Was your hypothesis correct? Summarize what you have found.

Change the Variables

You can vary this experiment in several ways. For example, feed the tadpoles different amounts of food and keep the temperature of the water constant. Then you can determine how food availability impacts their growth rate. Or you might feed them different kinds of vegetation.

Troubleshooter's Guide

Here are some problems that may arise during this experiment, some possible causes, and ways to remedy the problems.

Problem: All the tadpoles are going through metamorphosis at the same time.

Possible cause: The water temperatures are too similar. Find warmer and cooler places to put the jars.

Problem: Some of the tadpoles are dying.

Possible causes: They are not getting enough to eat, or the water is too warm, too cold, or too dirty. Try feeding tadpoles more or make the water a little warmer or cooler in the jars where tadpoles are dying. Also, change the water regularly.

You can also place different amounts of water in each container or a different number of tadpoles in each container. How does that affect their growth rate? Try varying the amount of sunlight that falls on each container. How does light affect tadpole growth?

Experiment 2
Insects: How does food supply affect the growth rate of grasshoppers or crickets?

Purpose/Hypothesis
WARNING: *You should be aware that it is illegal to release or dispose of live insects in certain areas. If you are not sure about performing this experiment, ask your science teacher.*

Insects such as grasshoppers and crickets go through an incomplete metamorphosis, where they gradually progress from eggs through several nymph stages to adulthood. In this experiment, you will explore how the amount of food available affects the growth rate of these insects from nymph to adulthood. Before you begin, make an educated guess about the outcome of this experiment based on your knowl-

What Are the Variables?

Variables are anything that might affect the results of an experiment. Here are the main variables in this experiment:

- the amount of food you supply
- the number of insects in each container
- the age and health of the eggs you begin with
- the temperature at which the insects are kept

In other words, the variables in this experiment are everything that might affect the time it takes the grasshoppers to develop into adults. If you change more than one variable, you will not be able to tell which variable had the most effect on the grasshoppers' growth rate.

edge of insects. This educated guess, or prediction, is your **hypothesis.** A hypothesis should explain these things:

- the topic of the experiment
- the variable you will change
- the variable you will measure
- what you expect to happen

A hypothesis should be brief, specific, and measurable. It must be something you can test through observation. Your experiment will prove or disprove your hypothesis. Here is one possible hypothesis for this experiment: "The more food supplied to grasshoppers, the faster they will become adults."

In this case, the **variable** you will change will be the amount of food you feed the grasshoppers, and the variable you will measure will be the time it takes them to become adults. You expect the grasshoppers that are fed the most food will become adults first.

Only one variable will change between the **control experiment** and the experimental containers, and that is the amount of food you supply. For the control, you will supply a medium amount of food. For the experimental insects, you will supply a greater and a lesser amount.

You will measure how many days it takes from the egg stage to the adult stage. If the insects in the containers with the most food grow fastest, your hypothesis is correct.

Level of Difficulty

Difficult, because of care required with live animals.

Materials Needed

- 3 glass jars with lids
- approximately 30 grasshopper or cricket eggs (You can obtain them from a biological supply company, such as those listed under For More Information.)
- fruit flies and a covered container to keep them in (You can also obtain fruit flies from a biological supply company.)
- measuring tape (with millimeters)

Approximate Budget

$30, if you need to purchase insects and food.

Timetable

2 to 3 weeks.

Step-by-Step Instructions

1. Place an equal amount of eggs in each of the three jars. Label the jars "medium/control," "small amount," and "large amount."

2. Place the jars in a warm, dry place out of the direct sun.

3. When the eggs hatch, record the day and time on a data chart similar to the one illustrated on page 353.

How to Experiment Safely

Always be careful with live animals and treat them with respect. Move their containers slowly. Wash your hands carefully before and after handling them. If any insects die, dispose of them. You should be aware that it is illegal to release or dispose of live insects in certain areas. If you are not sure about performing this experiment, ask your science teacher.

Step 1: Place an equal amount of eggs in each of the three jars. Label as shown.

Step 5: Measure the length of at least one insect in each group each day.

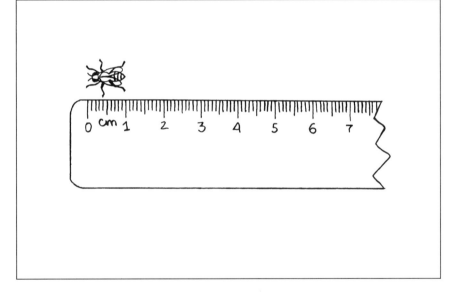

4. Provide the amount of food named on the jar labels to each group of nymphs. It will be difficult to count the fruit flies you supply, but try to record the approximate number you give to each group. Or you might vary the number of times you feed each group each day. Feed the small group only once, the control group twice, and the large group three times.

5. Every day record the growth of your insects. Measure the length of at least one insect in each group each day.

Hatching date: Control _____

Hatching date: Small Amount _____

Hatching date: Large Amount _____

Day

Jar	1 Size	2 Size	3 Size	4 Size	5 Size	6 Size	7 Size	8 Size
Control								
Small Amount								
Large Amount								

6. The supply house probably provided information about how large these insects will be as adults. When the insects in any group reach that size, release them in an appropriate area.

   You should be aware that it is illegal to release or dispose of live insects in certain areas. If you arc not sure about where to release your insects, ask your science teacher.

7. Continue feeding and measuring until all groups have reached adulthood.

Recording chart for Experiment 2.

Summary of Results

Study the results on your chart. How many days did it take your control group to reach adulthood? How many days did it take the group you fed the least? The most? Did food availability affect the growth rate of your insects? Was your hypothesis correct? Summarize what you have learned.

Troubleshooter's Guide

Here are some problems that may arise during this experiment, some possible causes, and ways to remedy the problems.

Problem: The growth rate of the insects in all the containers seemed about the same.

Possible cause: The amount you are feeding your insects is too similar. Try feeding one group several more times in a day than the other groups.

Problem: Many of the insects appear to be dying.

Possible cause: You are not feeding the insects enough, or the temperature is too cold. Try feeding more fruit flies, or check the information that came with the eggs to see if they need other kinds of food. Move them to a warmer place if the place you have been keeping them is rather cool.

Change the Variables

You can vary this experiment in several ways. For example, change the temperature where you keep the insects. How does heat or cold affect them? How about sunlight? Vary the number of eggs in each container. If some containers are very crowded, how does that affect the insects' growth rate? Check the labels that came with your eggs for the different kinds of food the insects eat. Does a different diet affect their growth rate?

 Design Your Own Experiment

How to Select a Topic Relating to this Concept

If you are interested in life cycles, you could study the different stages (eggs, larvae, nymphs) and the organisms' diets, habitats, sizes, forms, and activities. Perhaps you are interested in the transformation from caterpillars to butterflies. How long is each stage in the life cycle for various species? Where do they lay their eggs? What do they eat, if anything? Many butterflies, such as the monarch, migrate long distances. Where do they go? How can they fly so far, and how long do they stay there?

354 • Life Cycles

experiment
CENTRAL

Maybe you are more interested in the life cycles of amphibians, such as frogs, toads, salamanders, and newts. Investigate which ones live in your area and what time of the year you could best study the different stages of their life cycles.

Check the For More Information section and talk with your science teacher or school or community media specialist to start gathering information on animal life cycle questions that interest you.

Steps in the Scientific Method

To do an original experiment, you need to plan carefully and think things through. Otherwise, you might not be sure what question you are answering, what you are or should be measuring, or what your findings prove or disprove.

Here are the steps in designing an experiment:

- State the purpose of—and underlying question behind—the experiment you propose to do.
- Recognize the variables involved, and select one that will help you answer the question at hand.
- State a testable hypothesis, an educated guess about the answer to your question.
- Decide how to change the variable you selected.
- Decide how to measure your results.

Recording Data and Summarizing the Results

Your data should include charts, such as the ones you did for these experiments. They should be clearly labeled and easy to read. You may also want to include photos, graphs, or drawings of your experimental setup and results.

If you have done a nonexperimental project, explain clearly what your research question was and illustrate your findings.

Related Projects

Besides doing experiments, you could prepare a poster or model illustrating the life stages of a particular animal. Or you could research the migration patterns of a particular butterfly or study the effects of different stages of insects on agriculture. You could present your findings as a booklet, poster, or report. The possibilities are numerous.

For More Information

Goor, Ron, and Nancy Goor. *Insect Metamorphosis: From Egg to Adult.* New Jersey: Simon & Schuster, 1990. ❖ Discusses both complete and incomplete metamorphoses step-by-step with full color photographs.

Kneidel, Sally. *Creepy Crawlies and the Scientific Method.* Golden, CO: Fulcrum Resources, 1993. ❖ A series of informative chapters on insects and other small animals, experiments, and information on keeping those animals at home or school.

Ruiz, Andres Llamas, and Francisco Arredondo. *Metamorphosis (Cycles of Life Series).* New York: Sterling Publications, 1997. ❖ Details concepts and processes of metamorphosis, focusing on frogs, butterflies, and dragonflies with colorful illustrations.

Biological Supply Companies

Carolina Biological Supply Company
2700 York Rd
Burlington, NC 27215
1-800-334-5551

Frey Scientific
100 Paragon Parkway
Mansfield, OH 44903
1-800-225-FREY

Ward's Natural Science Establishment Inc.
5100 West Henrietta Rd
PO Box 92912
Rochester, NY 14692
1-800-962-2660

chapter 24

Properties of Light

Scholars wondered about the properties of light as early as 600 B.C. in Miletus, which was part of the Greek empire. We now know that **light** is a form of energy that travels through the universe in waves. All light energy exists in an **electromagnetic spectrum.** The **visible spectrum,** what we see as light, is part of the electromagnetic spectrum.

Experiments with a shutter

Isaac Newton (1642–1727), a brilliant English mathematician, had just received his bachelor's degree at the University of Cambridge when the bubonic plague hit Great Britain. Because the plague spread faster in cities, Newton continued his graduate studies for two years at his countryside home. During this time, he conducted many experiments. Early in 1666, Newton darkened his room and made a small hole in his shutters. After positioning a triangular glass prism in front of

Words to Know

Diffraction:
The bending of light or another form of electromagnetic radiation as it passes through a tiny hole or around a sharp edge.

Diffraction grating:
A device consisting of a surface into which are etched very fine, closely spaced grooves that cause different wavelengths of light to reflect or refract (bend) by different amounts.

Isaac Newton was the first to discover the spectrum of colors that exist in white light. (Library of Congress.)

experiment
CENTRAL

Words to Know

Electromagnetic spectrum:
The complete array of electromagnetic radiation, including radio waves (at the longest-wavelength end), microwaves, infrared radiation, visible light, ultraviolet radiation, X rays, and gamma rays (at the shortest-wavelength end).

Fluorescence:
The emission of visible light from an object when the object is bombarded with electromagnetic radiation, such as ultraviolet rays. The emission of visible light stops after the radiation source has been removed.

Hypothesis:
An idea phrased in the form of a statement that can be tested by observation and/or experiment.

Interference fringes:
Bands of color that fan out around an object.

this small beam of sunlight, he noticed a band of colors called a **spectrum.** He concluded that when the light hit the prism, it was bent, or **refracted,** to form many colors. He demonstrated how the colors in sunlight could be separated, then joined again to form white light.

In his work, Newton proved three of the most important characteristics of light: that it travels in straight lines, that it can be **reflected,** and that it can be refracted, or bent. Newton also did an experiment showing sunlight's reflection and refraction inside raindrops. He discovered that raindrops formed tiny transparent prisms that reflected and refracted the Sun to produce colorful rainbows.

Making waves

In 1801, Thomas Young, a London doctor, developed a theory that light traveled in waves and presented it to the Royal Society, a prestigious group of scientists. Christian Huygens of Holland had suggest-

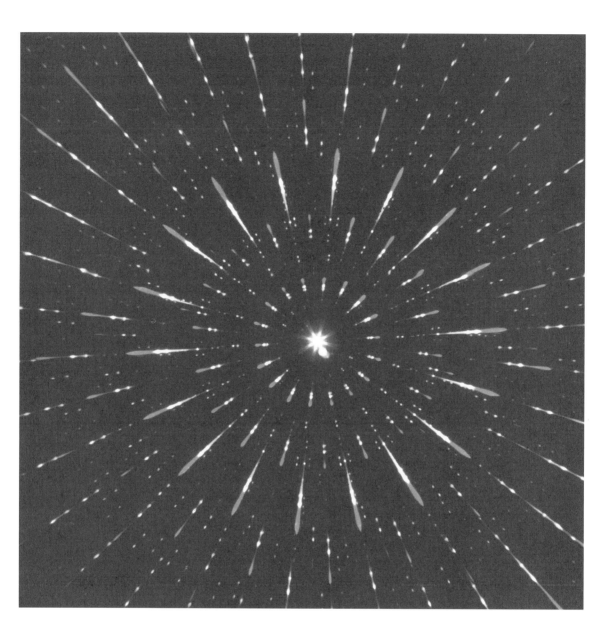

ed the presence of light waves in his book published in 1690, but Young would go on to prove it with his experiments in 1803.

Young used a screen with one slit. In front of that, he placed another screen with two side-by-side slits, and watched how sunlight passed through. What he saw was bands of color fanning out and meeting each other on the other side. Young realized these bands of color called **interference fringes** could be made only by waves of light.

This spectrum is produced by a modern diffraction grating. (Photo Researchers Inc. Reproduced by permission.)

experiment
CENTRAL

Up to that time it was thought that there was no form to light and that it existed everywhere. Young's experiment also showed **diffraction.** Diffraction occurs when an uninterruped wave of light hits an obstacle. The obstacle bends the wave into a shadow zone. This results in light and dark fringes outside the shadow's edge.

It glows in the dark

Some substances produce visible light if excited by **radiation,** such as invisible **ultraviolet** light. Visible light that is produced only when the radiation source is present is called **fluorescence.** Certain chemicals in laundry soaps react with sunlight to produce a fluorescence that makes clothes look brighter. Visible light that is produced even after the radiation source is removed is called **phosphorescence.** Some plants and animals in the sea produce a phosphorescence.

Great scientists throughout history came to their conclusions about light by experimenting. Conducting some projects will enable you to become familiar with some of light's properties.

Project 1
Looking for the Glow: Which objects glow under black light?

Purpose
Fluorescence is a scientific term that refers to something (usually a chemical compound) that reacts with light energy and glows brightly. In this project, you will examine compounds that react with ultraviolet light (UV), causing the compound to glow. When certain chemicals are exposed to UV light, the molecules absorb the light energy and then release it in the form of visible light.

Level of Difficulty
Easy/moderate.

Materials Needed
- UV light, also called a "black light" (fluorescent fixture with black or dark purple light bulb)
- Wisk or Woolite brand laundry detergent
- glow-in-the-dark plastic (can be a plastic toy)
- calcite (mineral found in nature or rock stores)
- white paper

Light:
A form of energy that travels in waves.

Phosphorescence:
The emission of visible light from an object when the object is bombarded with electromagnetic radiation, such as ultraviolet rays. The object stores part of the radiation energy and the emission of visible light continues for a period ranging from a fraction of a second to several days after the radiation source has been removed.

Radiation
Energy transmitted in the form of electromagnetic waves or subatomic particles.

Reflected:
The bouncing of light rays in a regular pattern off the surface of an object.

How to Work Safely

The chemicals in many detergents can irritate the skin, so avoid contact with the skin and eyes. Always use caution when handling household chemicals. Normally UV light is considered dangerous and harmful to the eyes. However, the fixture you are using emits very long wavelength UV, which is safe to use.

- objects to test (rocks and minerals, household detergents or cleaners, clothing, plants, etc.)

Approximate Budget
$20 for black light, $5 for detergents and for calcite.

Timetable
15 minutes.

Step-By-Step Instructions

1. Place the black light in a dark room and turn it on.

2. Place a small amount of Wisk or Woolite on a piece of white paper. Let the detergent dry a little and place the paper so that the light

LEFT: Detergent needed for Experiment 1.

RIGHT: Step 2: Place a small amount of Wisk or Woolite on a piece of white paper.

detergent
white paper

Category		
Detergents	Reacted	Color
Wisk	yes	blue green
Tide		
Woolite		
Era		
Minerals		
calcite	yes	orange / pink
gypsum		
quartz		
Flowers		
geraniums	yes	red lines in veins
roses		
four o'clocks		
Misc.		
eyeglasses	yes	green

Step 4: sample recording chart for Experiment 1.

shines on it. Notice the color of the chemical. Wisk is blue/green. Woolite is green/yellow.

3. Place different objects in front of the black light, such as white socks, white or colored towels, or blue jeans. Record any color you notice. Test groups of objects such as rocks, minerals, household detergents, flowers, fabric dyes, and plastic objects.

4. Repeat the test for each object. Record your observations.

experiment
CENTRAL

Troubleshooter's Guide

Here is a problem that may arise during this project, a possible cause, and a way to remedy the problem.

Problem: None of the objects emits light.

Possible cause: The black bulb should glow a dark purple when on. If the bulb is not glowing, the light is not working. Turn the lights on in the room and unplug the black light from the wall outlet. Check to see if the light bulb is firmly seated in its sockets on both ends. Repeat the project.

Summary of Results

Keep a record or chart of the results of the project. It's fun to discover how many things glow under UV light.

Project 2
Refraction and Defraction: Making a rainbow

Purpose

Rainbows are a good example of refraction. Water droplets are the first step in rainbow formation. The droplets form tiny transparent prisms that reflect and refract sunlight. Refraction or bending of sunlight, or white light, makes the spectrum colors of red, orange, yellow, green, blue, and violet spread out and become visible. Refraction can be made to occur in many transparent materials, including glass, plastic, or water.

In this project, you will use a special plastic material to display the different spectrums found in colored light. The plastic material is called a **diffraction grating**. A diffraction grating is a microscopically scratched plastic film that bends light as it goes *around* the scratched film, causing a spectrum to become visible.

Level of Difficulty

Easy/moderate.

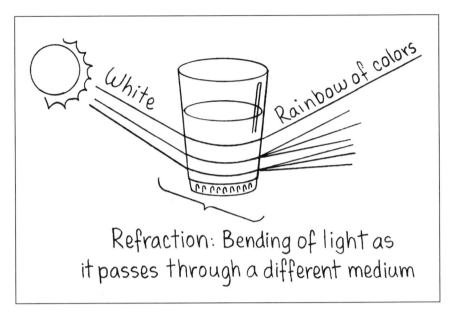

An example of light refraction using a glass of water.

Refraction: Bending of light as it passes through a different medium

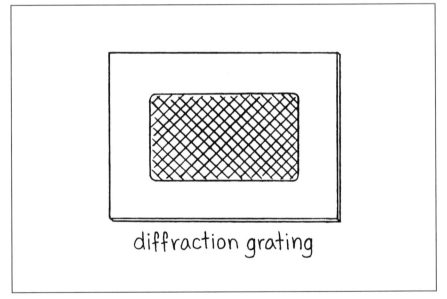

A diffraction grating is a microscopically scratched plastic film that bends light as it goes around the scratched film, causing a spectrum to become visible.

diffraction grating

Materials Needed

- diffraction grating (Local science and nature stores have these. They also may have toys called rainbow peepholes and rainbow makers, which contain diffraction gratings.)
- colored light bulbs (25-watt party lights in red, blue, green, yellow, purple, and orange.)
- white light bulb (any wattage)

How to Work Safely

Do not stick your fingers into the light sockets. Make sure the fixture is unplugged before removing the bulb. Do not touch hot bulbs.

- light fixture or lamp that fits light bulbs
- colored markers

Approximate Budget

$30: $4 to $5 for each bulb and $1 for a diffraction grating. (You might borrow colored Christmas lights.)

Timetable

Approximately 30 minutes to perform and record the results.

Step-By-Step Instructions

1. Insert the white light bulb into the lamp. Plug the lamp in and turn it on.

2. Turn off all other lights and darken the room as much as possible.

Step 4: Use the colored markers to draw the observed spectrum on a piece of paper and label it.

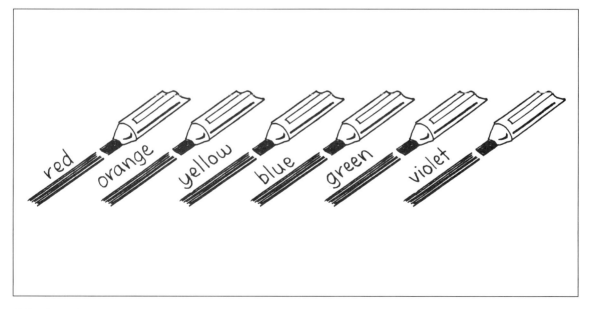

3. Hold the diffraction grating approximately 0.5 inch (1.25 cm) away from your eye and look through it.

4. Notice the colors of the visible spectrum. Use the colored markers to draw the spectrum on a piece of paper and label it.

5. Turn the lights back on, shut off the lamp, and allow the bulb to cool.

6. Unplug the lamp and remove the bulb.

7. Repeat Steps 1 through 6 with each colored light.

Summary of Results

Make a chart displaying the spectrums made by the different colored bulbs. Compare your results. Write a summary of your findings.

 Design Your Own Experiment

How to Select a Topic Relating to this Concept

There are many aspects of the properties of light you can study, either as a project or as an experiment. One aspect you may want to study might be reflection. If you choose reflection, one question might be: How can I see into a puddle past my reflection? Check the For More Information section for this topic, and talk with a teacher or with a librarian before finalizing your choice.

Steps in the Scientific Method

To do an original experiment, you need to plan carefully and think things through. Otherwise, you might not be sure what question you're answering, what you are or should be measuring, or what your findings prove or disprove.

Here are the steps in designing an experiment:

- State the purpose of—and the underlying question behind—the experiment you propose to do.
- Recognize the **variables** involved, and select one that will help you answer the question at hand.
- State a testable **hypothesis,** an educated guess about the answer to your question.

- Decide how to change the variable you selected.
- Decide how to measure your results.

Recording Data and Summarizing the Results
In the two properties of light projects, your data might include drawings or photographs. If you exhibit your project, you need to limit the amount of information you offer, so viewers will not be overwhelmed by detail. Make sure the beginning question, the variable you measured, the results and your conclusions about light are clear. Viewers and judges will want to see how each experiment was set up. You might want to take a detailed photo at each stage. Label your photos clearly. Have colorful tables and charts ready with information and results.

Related Projects
Your project does not have to be an experiment that investigates or answers a question. It can also be a model, such as Newton's original experiment with window shutters and a prism. Setting up such a model would be fun, and you would learn how this concept works.

For More Information
Buchwald, J.Z. *The Rise of the Wave Theory of Light.* Chicago: University of Chicago Press, 1989. ❖ Provides a history of this important concept.

Burnie, David. *Light.* London: Dorling Kindersley, 1992. ❖ Includes a chapter on how Newton split light and other interesting aspects of this phenomenon with great photos and illustrations.

Flatow, Irving. *Rainbows, Curve Balls and Other Wonders of the Natural World Explained.* New York: Morrow, 1988. ❖ Explains the concept of light in rainbows.

budget index

Under $5

Bold type indicates volume number.

budget index

Bold type indicates volume number.

$11—$15

$16—$20

$21—$25

$26—$30

$31—$35

budget index

Bold type indicates volume number.

level of difficulty index

Easy

Easy means that the average student should easily be able to complete the tasks outlined in the project/experiment, and that the time spent on the project is not overly restrictive.

Bold type indicates
volume number.

Easy/Moderate

Easy/Moderate means that the average student should have little trouble completing the tasks outlined in the project/experiment, and that the time spent on the project is not overly restrictive.

Moderate

*Moderate means that the average student should find tasks outlined in the
project/experiment challenging but not difficult, and that the time spent
project/experiment may be more extensive.*

Bold type indicates volume number.

Moderate/Difficult

Moderate/Difficult means that the average student should find tasks outlined in the project/experiment challenging, and that the time spent on the project/experiment may be more extensive.

Difficult

Difficult means that the average student will probably find the tasks outlined in the project/experiment mentally and physically challenging, and that the time spent on the project/experiment will be more extensive.

Bold type indicates volume number.

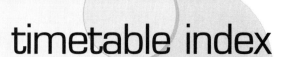

timetable index

experiment
CENTRAL

2 hours

Bold type indicates volume number.

experiment
CENTRAL

3-4 weeks

2 months

4 months

Bold type indicates volume number.

timetable index

6 months

experiment
CENTRAL

general index

Bold type indicates volume number; [ill.] indicates illustration or photograph.

Bold type indicates volume number.

general index

Bold type indicates volume number.

general index

Bold type indicates volume number.